CAMBRIDGE UNIVERSITY PRESS
Cambridge, New York, Melbourne, Madrid, Cape Town, Singapore, São Paulo, Delhi

Cambridge University Press
The Edinburgh Building, Cambridge CB2 8RU, UK

www.cambridge.org
Information on this title: www.cambridge.org/9780521736541

First published 2009

Janet McGiffin has asserted her right to be identified as the Author of the Work in
accordance with the Copyright, Design and Patents Act 1988.

Printed in India by Thomson Press (India) Limited
Typeset by Aptara Inc.

A catalogue record of this book is available from the British Library.

ISBN 978-0-521-73654-1 paperback
ISBN 978-0-521-73655-8 paperback plus 3 audio CDs

Contents

Characters

Dr. Maxine Cassidy: a doctor at Mercy Hospital ER

Shirley: the head nurse at Mercy Hospital ER

Detective Grabowski: a police officer; Maxine's friend

Dr. Leo Hochstedder: a specialist in lung diseases

Lillian Hochstedder: Leo's wife; an artist and co-owner of the Art Space

Helen Mueller: the business manager and co-owner of the Art Space

Louie: Maxine's neighbor; the owner of Louie's Antique Shop

Soren Berendorf: a famous artist

Wyoming Syzinski: an artist; Grabowski's friend

Rolondo: a gang leader

Rosa Jones: Rolondo's girlfriend

Latoya Thompson: Rolondo's neighbor

Officer Koranda: the night guard at the Police Crime Lab

Shirley's house

Lillian and Leo Hochstedder's house

W. Capitol Drive

Maxine's and Louie's apartment buiding

Fifth Street

27th Street

MILWAUKEE

Center Street

Apartment building of Rolondo, Rosa, Latoya

Helen Mueller's house

Mercy Hospital

Leo Hochstedder's medical office

The Art Space and Louie's Antique Shop

Lake Michigan

to Koranda's house

Central Police Station

C A N A D A

Lake Superior

Lake Huron

Police Crime Lab

WISCONSIN

Lake Michigan

Milwaukee

Detroit

Chicago

U.S.A.

N

Grabowski's house

Chapter 1 *Emergency!*

Dr. Maxine Cassidy sat down behind the reception desk at Mercy Hospital Emergency Room. She pulled out the lower desk drawer and put her feet on it. Her legs hurt. It was 8:00 p.m. on a Saturday night in August and she had been working in the ER for five long hours. Maxine was wearing surgical greens – a green cotton shirt and trousers. Maxine's short brown hair curled in the humid heat. The ER was air-conditioned, but whenever the automatic glass doors opened, the August heat of the Midwest United States came inside. And on Saturday night in the inner city of Milwaukee the door opened for a lot of sick or injured people.

Shirley, the ER head nurse, handed Maxine a glass of iced tea. "Four more hours and we can go home and cool off," she said.

Mercy Hospital was in the poorest, hottest, and most dangerous area of Milwaukee. Shirley owned a house in a neighborhood north of the inner city, where it was cooler because there were lots of trees. Maxine also lived in a neighborhood with lots of big trees. She rented an apartment on the northeast side, three blocks from Lake Michigan.

"I can't go home after work today," replied Maxine. "I'm going downtown to an art show at the Art Space. Dr. Hochstedder's wife, Lillian, is an artist and her statues are in the show. I promised Leo Hochstedder I would go. I've never met Lillian, but I've known Leo for years."

"After nine hours on your feet, you're going to stand around looking at art?" commented Shirley.

Maxine nodded. "Lillian's statues are very popular, according to Leo. Besides, a famous New York artist also has some work in the show and I want to see it. His name is Soren Berendorf."

"Never heard of him," said Shirley.

"Soren's collection is called *Wood Shapes*. I read in the newspaper that he attaches pieces of wood together into interesting shapes. One of them, *Musical Chairs,* costs a hundred thousand dollars."

"Don't buy anything, even if it costs one dollar!" ordered Shirley. "You need a new car! Your old one will die any day now."

Just then, Maxine's cellphone rang. She smiled when she read the caller ID: "Grabowski."

Maxine knew Detective Grabowski because the previous year he had been hurt in a car chase and a police ambulance had brought him to Mercy ER. After that, Maxine had seen a lot of Grabowski – dinners, movies, even midnight snacks at Tony's Fish Fries after she finished work. As a police detective, Grabowski often worked nights, like Maxine.

"Are we meeting for a snack tonight after work?" Maxine asked Grabowski.

"Sorry, but not tonight," said Grabowski. "I'm at the Art Space working as a private detective at a show. The owner wants to make sure that the art is safe. It's very valuable. I don't make much money as a police detective, you know, and off-duty work pays well."

"What a coincidence! I'm coming to the Art Space after work," said Maxine. "We can meet there."

"Then you can meet a friend of mine too," replied Grabowski. "That is, if he shows up. I'm worried about him. A week ago he said he would meet me tonight. But he's not here yet and he hasn't called me either."

"Maybe he's just late," suggested Maxine.

"It's not like him. In fact, he hasn't called me in a week," continued Grabowski. "We grew up together in Milwaukee, then he moved away for several years. He just came back. He stayed with me for a week, then he moved to his own apartment. I don't have his address or phone numbers. I'm worried that he's hurt or sick. I think I should call the hospitals in Milwaukee to see if they have any record of him. His mother is worried and so am I."

"I'll check the Mercy Hospital computer," said Maxine. "What's his name?"

"Wyoming Syzinski."

Maxine checked the computer patient records. "No, Wyoming Syzinski hasn't come to Mercy Hospital." She said goodbye to Grabowski and closed her cellphone.

Shirley smiled at Maxine. "Are you seeing that good-looking Polish detective tonight?"

"Grabowski is working as a private detective at the art show. I'll see him there, for a few minutes at least."

"That's what you get for falling in love with a police detective. They're always working." Shirley smiled.

"I'm not in love," said Maxine, but she smiled back.

At that moment the doors to the ER opened and Rolondo walked in. Rolondo was the leader of an inner-city gang. As usual, he was wearing expensive high-fashion clothing – blue silk shirt, yellow trousers, and Italian shoes.

Shirley didn't like Rolondo. She put her hands on her broad hips. "Get out of here, Rolondo! You don't look sick!" Shirley was a big woman who could handle any trouble, including the leader of a street gang.

"A woman who lives in my building is sick," said Rolondo. "She's outside in my car. Remember Latoya Thompson, Dr. Maxine? She lives with my girlfriend, Rosa. Latoya has come to the ER several times."

"I remember Latoya," said Maxine. "Bring her inside."

"She's too sick to walk," said Rolondo.

"I'll get a wheelchair," said Shirley.

Shirley took a wheelchair outside, and she and Rolondo brought Latoya into the ER. Maxine and Shirley helped her to lie down on a bed. But before Maxine could talk to Latoya, the doors of the ER opened and an emergency medical technician from an ambulance hurried in.

"I've got two people in my ambulance who have been shot!" said the EMT. "They need help, fast!"

Maxine put a blanket over Latoya. She said to Rolondo, "I'm sorry, but Latoya will have to wait while I take care of these two people."

Chapter 2 *Wyoming is hurt*

Shirley and the EMT brought in the two people from the ambulance. The man was wearing jeans and a white T-shirt. The woman was wearing a red miniskirt and a tight purple blouse.

"Rosa!" shouted Rolondo. He grabbed the hand of the woman wearing the red miniskirt. "Dr. Maxine, this is my girlfriend, Rosa Jones."

Maxine examined the girl. She had been shot, but she was awake. "What happened, Rosa?" she asked.

"I was standing in front of our building talking to our new neighbor. Two men drove by in a car and shot us!" Rosa replied.

"Did you see their faces?" asked Rolondo.

"Yes," said Rosa. But then she closed her eyes.

"Talk later." Maxine put a needle in Rosa's arm.

Shirley opened the man's shirt. "He's bleeding a lot, but he's still breathing," she said. "What's this man's name, Rolondo?"

"I don't know. He moved into our building only last week."

Shirley reached into the man's pocket and took out his wallet. "Wyoming Syzinski, it says on his driver's license."

"Grabowski's friend!" said Maxine.

Shirley called the surgery unit to let them know that two patients with gunshot wounds were in the ER and needed surgery. Quickly two nurses arrived to take them to surgery.

Maxine and Shirley went to examine Latoya. Rolondo followed them.

"Latoya is getting worse," said Shirley.

Maxine put her hand on Latoya's forehead. It was cold and damp with sweat. "Can you hear me?" Maxine asked.

Latoya didn't answer.

"When did she get sick?" Maxine asked Rolondo.

"About five o'clock this afternoon," replied Rolondo.

Maxine put her hand on Latoya's wrist to feel her pulse. Her heartbeat was faint and she wasn't breathing well either.

"What's wrong with her?" Rolondo asked Maxine.

Maxine shook her head, worried. "I don't know. It's unusual for someone to get this sick so fast. What did she eat today?"

"I don't know," said Rolondo.

Maxine and Shirley pumped everything out of Latoya's stomach. Shirley put some into a bottle and sent it to the lab to find out what Latoya had eaten. Then Maxine gave her drugs to raise her blood pressure. But suddenly Latoya stopped breathing and her heart stopped beating.

Immediately Shirley called for help. Other doctors and nurses quickly arrived with emergency equipment and medicines, but they could do nothing to save Latoya.

"You waited too long to take care of Latoya!" Rolondo said to Maxine. "Latoya shouldn't have died!"

Maxine felt terrible. "I don't know why she died," she said to Rolondo.

Then Shirley handed Maxine a paper. "This is from the lab – the test results from Latoya's stomach."

Maxine read the report and told the others, "Latoya had eaten a lot of chocolate. And there was also medicine for TB – tuberculosis – in her stomach, INH."

Rolondo looked surprised. "Latoya didn't have TB."

"Then why did she take INH?" asked Maxine.

Rolondo lifted his shoulders in a shrug. "I don't know."

"Could Latoya have died from taking too much INH?" asked Shirley.

"I'll ask Dr. Hochstedder," said Maxine. "He's a specialist in lung diseases and has had many TB patients. He's at the Art Space now with his wife, but he always carries his cellphone."

Maxine called Leo Hochstedder. "Can a person die from taking too much INH?" Maxine asked. She read the lab report to him.

"Yes, someone could die from taking that much INH," Leo answered. "I hope this isn't one of my TB patients!"

"Her name was Latoya Thompson. She lived on Fifth Street and Center Street," said Maxine.

"I don't remember that name," said Leo. "Maybe she's a patient at the Milwaukee Health Department TB Clinic."

"Latoya's friend says that she didn't have TB," said Maxine. "But I'm going to order an autopsy to find out." She thanked Leo and closed her cellphone.

"An autopsy?" asked Rolondo. He had been listening to the conversation.

"The Mercy Hospital pathologist will examine Latoya's body to find the cause of death," explained Maxine. "Autopsies aren't common because a lot of tests are done before a person dies, so the cause of death is usually known. But Latoya died too quickly to have many tests.

I'll ask the pathologist to test for TB. But an autopsy doesn't always give the right answer to why a person has died. It would help the pathologist if we knew more about Latoya."

"Such as what she ate today," suggested Shirley.

"Rolondo," said Maxine, "will you take me to Latoya's apartment tonight? I want to search for any food that had gone bad."

"Sure," said Rolondo. "It's not far. I'll take you in my Cadillac."

Shirley frowned at Maxine. "You're crazy to go there, especially at night, and especially with Rolondo! There could be trouble!"

"I want to find out why Latoya died," argued Maxine. "I want to make sure I did everything I could to help her."

"Then I'm coming with you," decided Shirley. "Nobody makes trouble with me. But we're not going in Rolondo's Cadillac because another gang might shoot at it. We'll take your old car and hope it doesn't die!"

Rolondo sat down in the ER waiting room. "I'll stay here until Rosa is out of surgery and I know she's OK."

Shirley brought him a cup of coffee.

An hour later, the surgeon called. "Rosa and Wyoming are out of surgery," he reported. "Rosa is doing well, but they are both still unconscious."

Maxine hung up and told Rolondo the good news. "Rosa and Wyoming will be moved to the ICU now – the Intensive Care Unit," she told him. "You can see Rosa there."

"When Rosa wakes up, she can tell me who shot her," said Rolondo. He got himself another cup of coffee.

"It was probably a gang shooting," said Shirley. "Other gangs are always shooting at you and your friends."

Rolondo nodded. "That's true. The police don't even investigate the shootings any more."

At midnight Rolondo agreed to take Maxine and Shirley to Latoya's apartment. They went outside to the parking lot. Rolondo got into his white Cadillac. Shirley and Maxine got into Maxine's yellow Nissan.

"It's hot in here!" complained Shirley, as Maxine drove out of the parking lot. "Turn on your air conditioner!"

"It's broken. And now a red light is on," said Maxine with a worried frown.

"That means that your engine is too hot," said Shirley. "You need a new car."

"I'm saving money to buy a house," said Maxine. She watched the red light nervously as she drove behind Rolondo's white Cadillac through the dark streets of the inner city. Suddenly, a few blocks from Fifth Street, the engine died and smoke rose from the front of the car. It rolled to a stop.

"Don't stop here!" shouted Shirley. "We'll be robbed!"

Maxine pulled out her cellphone. "I'll call 911 and a police officer will come." She was trying to remain calm.

But before Maxine could phone the emergency number, 911, Rolondo had backed up his Cadillac. "Get in," he said. "Leave your car here. I'll tell my friends to steal everything out of it, and you can buy a new car with the insurance money."

"Don't tell Grabowski," said Maxine to Shirley.

The street where Rolondo lived had been beautiful many years before, when it was a middle-class neighborhood.

However, the area had gone downhill and now the people who lived there didn't have enough money to paint their houses. The steps to Rolondo's apartment building were broken and bottles lay where flowers used to grow. The lobby light had burnt out. Maxine and Shirley followed Rolondo up the dark stairs. He opened the door to an apartment on the second floor.

Maxine, Shirley, and Rolondo searched the apartment for bad food, but they didn't find any. In the bedroom Maxine found a red box of chocolates. There were only three chocolates left.

"Where did these chocolates come from?" Maxine asked Rolondo.

"How should I know?" he replied. "Latoya was always eating chocolates."

Maxine put the box under her arm. "Can you take me to the Art Space?" she asked Rolondo.

"And after that please take me home," added Shirley.

"OK," said Rolondo. "And then I'm going back to Mercy Hospital. I want to be there when Rosa wakes up. I want to know who shot her!"

Chapter 3   *Falling chairs!*

Rolondo dropped Maxine at the Art Space. Hundreds of people were inside, talking, eating, and drinking. Maxine heard someone playing the piano. Everyone was wearing expensive clothes and jewelry. Maxine felt uncomfortable in her cotton dress and sensible shoes. But she was hungry, so she went to the food table and had some smoked salmon and olives while she looked around.

Soren Berendorf's collection *Wood Shapes* was arranged around the large room. They were smooth shapes of wood painted different colors. The largest shape hung by a rope over the center of the room. It was made of twelve chairs tied together. Each chair was painted a different color. A thick rope went up from the chairs to a large hook in the ceiling. Then the rope went down to the floor, where it was tied to a hook by the food table.

The chairs hung above a grand piano, where a man with black hair was playing. As he played, the chairs slowly turned. A blonde woman wearing a tight green dress was leaning against the piano drinking from a tall glass. Another glass sat on the piano near the man.

Just then Maxine spotted her neighbor Louie. Louie lived in the apartment below Maxine and owned an antique shop next door to the Art Space. Louie was wearing yellow trousers, a pink shirt with a purple scarf and black shoes. He was standing near the man playing the piano and looking around the room as if he were searching for someone. He had a worried frown on his face.

"Louie!" Maxine called. She pushed through the crowd and put her hand on his arm.

"What are you doing here?" asked Louie, kissing her cheek.

"Leo Hochstedder invited me. He wants me to see his wife's statues. Also, I'm looking for Grabowski. Have you seen him?" Louie knew Grabowski because they had met at Maxine's apartment.

"Maybe Grabowski is with Helen. I need to talk to her. They might be upstairs," Louie replied. He pointed at some wide steps that went up to the second level.

"Who's Helen?" asked Maxine.

"Helen Mueller is the business manager of the Art Space, and a very powerful woman. She talked Soren Berendorf into bringing his collection here. That's a real success!" Louie looked up at the chairs hanging above them. He waved at the man playing the piano. "Soren!" he called. "Come upstairs with me! Take a break from playing the piano."

Soren shook his head. He kept playing.

Maxine stared at Soren. He closed his eyes and leaned his forehead against the piano, as if he were falling asleep. "He looks very tired," Maxine said.

Louie looked worried. "Soren has been working hard."

Maxine looked up at the slowly moving chairs. "I hope that rope is strong enough!" she joked.

Louie bit his lips. "I hope so too. It's made of three ropes twisted together." He called again to Soren and the blonde woman. "Soren! Lillian! Come upstairs with me!"

The blonde woman looked at Louie, but didn't move. She took a drink from her glass, then put it down on the piano. But the glass was too close to the edge and it fell off.

"Is that Lillian Hochstedder, Leo's wife?" Maxine asked.

"Yes. Her work is upstairs," said Louie. "Lillian, you should be near your statues. People will be asking questions about them."

"Soren needs me," replied Lillian.

Louie took Lillian's arm. "Then make Soren come upstairs with you."

"He won't leave the piano. He says that the piano music is part of *Musical Chairs*." Lillian looked up at the chairs. Then she suddenly changed her mind. "OK, I'll come with you. I want to talk to Helen," she said. "I think she's upstairs."

Maxine followed Louie and Lillian, leaving Soren alone at the piano. The stairs to the second floor were crowded with people sitting on the steps, chatting, eating from small plates, and drinking from plastic glasses. On the second floor was a large room where people were looking at a collection of strange statues. The statues were twelve life-size heads sitting on tall platforms. Each head was painted white, brown or black.

"This is my work," said Lillian proudly to Maxine. "The heads are made of clay. The eyes are glass and the teeth are shells."

"They look like real people!" exclaimed Maxine.

Lillian smiled. "They do, don't they? They're very popular. But Soren says I'm not a real artist. Helen doesn't like them either. But I'm Helen's business partner and she has to put my statues in the show."

Maxine spotted Lillian's husband, Leo Hochstedder, talking to a tall man with thick black hair. Maxine waved at Leo, but he didn't notice. He and the man left the room.

Louie pointed at a tall, beautiful woman with smooth black hair and a red dress. "Helen!" Louie hurried over and said something quietly to her.

Helen pushed Louie away. "That's impossible," she said.

"Come downstairs and see for yourself," said Louie.

Helen shook her head. Then Lillian grabbed Helen's arm and began whispering in her ear.

"Impossible!" replied Helen. She turned her back.

"Let's find Grabowski," Louie said to Maxine. "I need to talk to him, but I don't see him up here."

At the top of the stairs Maxine paused to look for Grabowski in the crowd below and spotted him near the food table. She waved at him. Grabowski waved back and Maxine and Louie hurried down the steps. It was so crowded that it took them nearly ten minutes to reach the table.

"Grabowski, I found Wyoming!" Maxine called when she got near him.

But Louie pushed in front of her. "Grabowski, I have to talk to you!"

"Let's go where it's quiet." Grabowski pointed toward the kitchen.

Maxine started to walk toward the kitchen, but her foot hit something. She nearly fell. At that same moment she heard a loud sharp sound. "What's that noise?" she asked Louie.

"It's the rope!" Louie pointed a shaking finger at *Musical Chairs*. The rope that held the chairs up was breaking.

The three ropes twisted together were breaking one by one. *Musical Chairs* dropped a little.

"Get away from the piano!" Grabowski shouted to Soren.

But Soren didn't even look up. He kept playing the piano. The sharp sound came again. Then the rope broke. With a huge crash, *Musical Chairs* fell onto the piano and onto Soren Berendorf.

Chapter 4   *The rope broke?*

"Call an ambulance, Maxine!" shouted Grabowski. "I'm calling for more police." He took out his cellphone.

Maxine took out her phone and dialed 911. She gave her name and the address of the Art Space. Then she knelt by Soren Berendorf.

Louie and Grabowski were helping people lift *Musical Chairs* off Soren. Maxine put her cheek near Soren's face. She could feel his breath on her cheek, but he was breathing very slowly. She put her fingers on his wrist. His heart was beating, although his pulse was weak. She didn't want to move him in case he'd injured his neck or back.

"Soren!" Maxine called loudly. "Can you hear me?"

Soren didn't answer.

Helen dropped to her knees next to Maxine. Leo Hochstedder knelt beside Helen. "He looks bad," said Leo.

"His heart is beating all right," said Maxine. "But his breathing is much slower than normal."

Helen started to cry. "Soren will say *Musical Chairs* fell because of me! My insurance will be canceled! No other artist will bring their work here! The Art Space is ruined!"

"Don't worry," said Leo Hochstedder, but he looked worried himself.

In a few minutes an ambulance arrived and two EMTs lifted Soren into it. The driver took out his notebook. "His name?" he asked.

Louie answered. Tears ran down his cheeks. "Soren Berendorf. He's a famous artist!"

"And does this famous artist have health insurance?" asked the driver.

"I'll pay the hospital," said Helen. She started to cry.

More police officers arrived. Grabowski called the Central Police Station and the captain put him on the case as the lead detective. He and the other officers began asking questions and taking names. A police photographer took photos of *Musical Chairs* and the rope, which had broken near the floor by the food table.

When the photographer had finished, Grabowski put the rope into a plastic bag. "Take this to the Crime Lab," he told another officer. "Get them to find out why it broke. And tell the guests to leave, except the owners of the Art Space."

Maxine looked at Grabowski. "Just before the rope broke," she said, "I hit my foot against something. I think it was the rope. Maybe it broke when I fell over it."

Louie was standing nearby. He shook his head. "You couldn't break that rope. It's new. I bought it yesterday."

"Which store?" Grabowski took out his notebook.

"The hardware store on the corner," said Louie.

"Who hung *Musical Chairs* up there?" demanded Grabowski.

"Soren, Helen, Lillian, Leo, and me," Louie answered. "Soren put the rope through the hook on the ceiling. Then we all pulled on the rope to raise it to the right height. It was really heavy. Soren tied the rope to the hook on the floor himself."

"Did you use all the rope that you bought?" asked Grabowski.

"No. The rest is in the garage," answered Louie.

"Show me," ordered Grabowski.

Louie led the way, followed by Grabowski, Maxine, and Helen. The door to the garage was in the office. Lillian was in the office lying on a couch and Leo was sitting by her. He looked at Grabowski. "I saw you here all evening," he said. "I didn't know you were a police officer."

Helen said, "I hired Detective Grabowski as a private detective to make sure that Soren's art was safe."

"You didn't do a good job, did you?" said Leo to Grabowski. He looked at his watch. "Can we go home?"

"Not yet." Grabowski opened the door to the garage.

He turned on the light and went down the stairs. Helen, Louie, and Maxine followed. Leo and Lillian went down the stairs too.

The garage was in the basement below the Art Space. Three cars were parked there: a blue Lexus, a silver Prius, and a small green Ford pick-up truck. Against the wall was a table with paints and brushes. Next to it were three big wooden boxes.

"This garage is for the Art Space and my antique shop," Louie explained to Grabowski. "Helen, Lillian, and I park our cars here, and this is where I repair my antiques." He went to the table and pointed to some rope. "That's the rest of the rope and the receipt from the store."

Grabowski put both in a plastic bag. "How do you open the main garage door to drive inside?" he asked.

"It's an electric door that opens with a code." Louie pointed to a keypad on the wall.

"Who knows the code?" asked Grabowski.

"Helen, Lillian, Leo, and me." Louie typed four numbers into the keypad and the garage door rose. Outside, a narrow road went up to a side street. Louie pushed a button and the garage door closed.

Grabowski pointed to some stairs on the far side of the garage. "Where do those stairs go?" he asked.

"To the kitchen of my shop," answered Louie. "Helen has a key to that door, and I have a key to the door to the Art Space."

"Now can we go home?" repeated Leo Hochstedder.

Grabowski nodded. "But after you leave, I'm locking the Art Space. Nobody can come in until I say. A police officer will guard the door."

"When can I get back inside?" demanded Helen. "Tomorrow the food company needs to get its tables."

"I'll tell you tomorrow morning," said Grabowski.

Leo and Lillian Hochstedder got into their Lexus, Helen got into her Prius, and Louie got into his little green Ford pick-up. They drove off and Grabowski closed the garage door. Then he took Maxine's arm and they went up the stairs and out the front door of the Art Space. A police officer locked the door behind them.

"Tell me about Wyoming while I walk you to your car," said Grabowski.

"My car died tonight," said Maxine. "I left it parked on the street."

Grabowski took out his cellphone. "I'll call the police truck to get it. Where is it?"

"On Center Street, a few blocks west of Fifth Street," Maxine said.

Grabowski looked at her sharply. "What were you doing there? You could have gotten into real trouble!"

"I was perfectly safe. I was with Shirley and Rolondo," said Maxine.

"Are you crazy?" shouted Grabowski. "Rolondo is the leader of a gang!"

"I know," said Maxine. "Can you give me a ride home? Where's your car?"

Grabowski pointed at a small red rental car. "My new Ford Taurus X was stolen yesterday," he said, frowning. "From right in front of my house!"

Maxine got into Grabowski's rental car. She told him about Wyoming, Rosa, and Latoya.

Grabowski sighed. "Wyoming probably got shot in Rolondo's gang wars," he said. "How badly is he hurt?"

"Badly. When I left the hospital, he was unconscious. But he was breathing well and his heart was beating normally. He's a strong healthy man, so he should recover quickly." Maxine stopped talking. Many things could go wrong and it was better not to talk about them.

"I'll call his mother," said Grabowski.

"Wyoming has lost a lot of blood," Maxine continued. "He needs someone to give blood for him. It's safer if we know who's giving blood. It's also a lot cheaper."

"I will," said Grabowski. "I gave blood for Wyoming when he had a car accident, when we were teenagers. I'll go to Mercy Hospital now."

Grabowski drove Maxine home through the cool, tree-shaded neighborhoods of the east side of Milwaukee. He kissed her, and watched her unlock her front door and go inside. Then he drove to Mercy Hospital to give blood for his friend.

Chapter 5   *Why is Louie so nervous?*

The next morning was Sunday. Maxine was still sleeping at 10:00 when the phone rang. It was Grabowski.

"I'm at the Central Police Station," Grabowski said. "Soren's dead."

Maxine couldn't believe her ears. "I should have gone with him in the ambulance," said Maxine. "His injuries must have been very serious. EMTs are well trained, but Soren needed a doctor."

"You did the best you could," said Grabowski.

"Grabowski, do you think that I damaged the rope? I hit my foot against something just before the rope broke."

"You didn't damage the rope," replied Grabowski. "I've read the report from the Crime Lab. The rope was cut – and with a very sharp knife. It wasn't an accident."

"It was such a thick rope!" remembered Maxine.

"The rope was made of three smaller ropes twisted together. Someone cut one of the smaller ropes. The other two could have broken any time that evening."

"Then that's murder!" Maxine said.

"Only if the person who cut the rope knew that Soren Berendorf would be sitting under *Musical Chairs* when the rope broke," replied Grabowski. "I'm going to the Art Space now to search for sharp knives. I'll also search Louie's Antique Shop."

"Louie didn't cut that rope. He talks too much to carry out a serious crime," said Maxine.

"But several people saw Louie touching the rope during the show," said Grabowski. "I phoned Louie and told him to meet me at his antique shop. He needs to explain why he was touching the rope. And I want him to show me how he, Helen, Lillian, and Soren hung the chairs above the piano. Maybe that's when the rope was cut."

"Isn't it strange that Soren Berendorf didn't move when the rope broke?" Maxine commented. "You shouted at him to get away from the piano, but he didn't move."

"Soren had been drinking a lot, according to the people I talked to," replied Grabowski. He then changed the subject. "Last night I gave blood for Wyoming. Then I went to see him. He's still unconscious. Why won't he wake up?"

"He lost a lot of blood so he's weak. And the medicine they're giving him for the pain is making him sleep," Maxine explained. "How is Rosa?"

"She's conscious, but she sleeps a lot," replied Grabowski.

Maxine hung up the phone and went outside to get her newspaper off the front steps. There was an article about Soren on the front page. The shooting of Wyoming Syzinski and Rosa Jones was on the back page. There was no personal information about Rosa, but the article said that Wyoming was a well-known artist who had had many shows in California, Arizona, and other western states.

Just then, Louie tapped on her door. He was scratching his arms and his neck. The skin was red.

"What's the matter?" asked Maxine.

"I'm a sensitive person. Seeing *Musical Chairs* fall on Soren gave me an allergy. My skin itches."

"I'll phone the drugstore and tell them to give you some medicine," said Maxine. "But only take two pills every four hours."

Louie dropped into a chair and held a handkerchief to his eyes. "Soren Berendorf died. Helen just phoned me."

Maxine put her hand on his arm. "Grabowski told me. Did you know Soren well?"

"No, I only met him three days ago. But I helped him unpack his entire collection and arrange it in the Art Space. I helped him put *Musical Chairs* together and hang it over the piano. I even brought him drinks during the show!"

"You helped him a lot," said Maxine.

"Soren never even thanked me!" Louie said angrily. He scratched his arms. "And now Grabowski wants to talk to me again. I'm being punished for being so nice to Soren!" Louie scratched his neck.

"Grabowski is only trying to find out why the rope broke," said Maxine.

Louie bit his nails. "The truth is that Soren Berendorf hardly spoke to me. I wasn't important. Soren only liked money."

After Louie left, Maxine thought about Wyoming and Soren. Both were artists born in Milwaukee, and both had returned to Milwaukee recently. Did they know each other? Maxine wondered. She looked at her watch. It was time to get dressed for work. But then she remembered that she had no car. She had to get to Mercy Hospital without one.

Chapter 6 *Someone cut the rope*

After Grabowski finished speaking to Maxine, he drove to Louie's Antique Shop. It was a quiet Sunday morning and the shops there were closed. Grabowski parked his rental car in front of the shop. He tried the front door. Locked. Grabowski banged on the door. Just then Louie hurried up the sidewalk.

"Sorry I'm late, Detective," Louie gasped. "I ran to the drugstore for medicine. I'm a sensitive person and my skin itches when I'm under stress. Look, my arms are all red!"

Grabowski looked away.

Louie unlocked the door and turned on the air conditioner. "Would you like some cool mint tea?" he offered. "Perhaps an iced cappuccino?"

Grabowski ignored the offer. "Sit down, Louie," he said. "I have bad news for you. The Police Crime Lab tested the rope that held *Musical Chairs.* Someone cut one of the three smaller ropes. That's why it broke."

"Oh no!" Louie put his hand over his mouth.

"Do you know who might have cut that rope, Louie?" asked Grabowski.

"I have no idea at all!" Louie scratched his arms.

"Did you see anyone near the rope?" asked Grabowski.

"Of course! Hundreds of people!" said Louie. "The rope came down to the floor right by the food table."

"Some people told me you were touching the rope during the show," said Grabowski. "Why?"

Louie scratched his arms even more. "I was checking that it was tied tightly," he said.

Grabowski wondered why Louie was so nervous. "You helped put *Musical Chairs* together, you helped hang it, and you stood by Soren at the piano," he said. "Why?"

Louie's eyes filled with tears. "I liked Soren, at first. But Soren ignored me and all I did for him!"

"So you got very angry at Soren. You cut the rope so *Musical Chairs* would fall on him," said Grabowski. "That's why you were near the rope, and why you waited near the piano."

"No!" Louie shouted.

"How many drinks did you bring Soren? Did you want him to drink so much that he would sit at the piano until the chairs fell on him?"

"No! No! I only brought Soren three drinks!" shouted Louie. "Ask Helen. She poured them and told me to take them to Soren."

Grabowski wrote in his notebook. "Now tell me what you know about Helen and Lillian."

Louie took a deep breath. "Helen and Lillian grew up in wealthy families on the northeast side of Milwaukee near Lake Michigan. They both married rich doctors. After about twenty years Helen got divorced. Lillian is still married to Dr. Leo Hochstedder."

"Why did Helen and Lillian open the Art Space?" asked Grabowski.

"Lillian used to be a good artist. She had many good paintings to sell and Helen is very smart with money. So Helen and Lillian opened the Art Space with Lillian as the artist and Helen as the business manager. At first, Lillian's paintings sold well. Then, about two years ago, Lillian's work went downhill and her paintings stopped selling. So Helen invited other artists to put their work in the Art Space. Helen moved Lillian's paintings upstairs. Lillian and Helen started having a lot of fights. I could hear them from the kitchen of my shop. They shouted at each other!"

"What were they fighting about?" asked Grabowski.

"Helen was tired of being partners with Lillian. She wanted to own the Art Space by herself. She wanted to have all the money the business made for herself and only pay Lillian fifty percent from the sale of her paintings."

Grabowski wrote that in his notebook. "How did Helen and Lillian get along with Soren Berendorf?" asked Grabowski.

"Lillian hated him," replied Louie immediately.

"Why?" asked Grabowski.

"Soren told Lillian that her statues of heads weren't art. He told her she should just be the wife of a wealthy doctor. Lillian cried."

"But Lillian helped Soren hang *Musical Chairs*," Grabowski commented.

"Helen told Lillian that she was a business partner and she had to help. Her husband, Leo, helped too."

"I noticed that Lillian stood next to the piano near Soren for a long time," said Grabowski. "Why would she stay there if she hated Soren?"

"It's a mystery to me, Detective," said Louie, scratching his arms.

Grabowski shook his head, puzzled. "Soren was popular in New York and London. Why would he put his collection in a small show in Milwaukee?"

"Because Helen helped Soren when he was poor," Louie explained. "When Soren was just starting out in Milwaukee, Helen and her rich friends bought his work. Then when she wanted good artists for the Art Space, Helen called Soren in New York. She begged him to bring his latest collection to the Art Space. Soren's work would make the Art Space a real success."

"And Soren could sell more of his art," said Grabowski.

Louie nodded. "So Soren came to Milwaukee. But three days before the show Soren and Helen had a big fight. I could hear them screaming at each other. Helen said she would kill him!"

"What was the fight about?" asked Grabowski.

Louie bit his nails. "Soren wanted to break the agreement he had signed with Helen. He wanted more money, but Helen refused. So Soren shouted that he would take his collection back to New York."

"What did Helen say?" asked Grabowski.

"Helen screamed that she would stop him, no matter what she had to do."

Chapter 7 *Soren had enemies*

At that moment Helen walked in. "Morning, Detective," she said with a cool nod.

Grabowski had been too busy to really look at Helen the previous night, but now he saw that she was very beautiful. Her gray trousers and pink jacket fitted her slim body like a glove. As she came nearer he could smell the perfume from her smooth black hair. But her hands were shaking and she had dark shadows under her eyes. She looked exhausted.

Helen sat down and closed her eyes. "Louie, please bring me an iced cappuccino. I didn't sleep all night. Every time I closed my eyes, I saw Soren's body under those awful chairs."

But now coffee was the last thing on Louie's mind. "Somebody cut the rope holding up the chairs," he cried. "But how? We all checked the rope before the show. Remember? I checked, you checked, Lillian checked. Even Leo checked the rope very carefully."

"And I thought things couldn't get any worse," Helen groaned.

"I'm searching this shop and the Art Space again," said Grabowski. "And your cars. You stay here."

"Look wherever you want," sighed Helen, handing over her car keys. Louie also gave Grabowski his car keys.

Grabowski searched Louie's kitchen first. He found several sharp knives, which he put in plastic bags. He went down to the garage. Louie's green pick-up truck and Helen's silver

Prius were there. So were the three large wooden boxes that had been there the previous evening. Grabowski opened them. They were all empty.

Grabowski unlocked the cars and looked inside. He found nothing sharp.

He went up the steps to the Art Space. In the kitchen were several large knives, which Grabowski put into plastic bags. Then he searched the rest of the rooms. Nothing had changed from the previous night, except that the left-over food smelled terrible. The police had roped off the piano and *Musical Chairs* so that no one could go near them. Grabowski went back to Louie's shop.

"You can go into the Art Space now," Grabowski told Helen, "but stay away from the piano and the chairs."

Helen went back to her office in the Art Space. Grabowski followed. She sat down at her computer. "Can I check my email? Or do you want to search inside my computer, too?"

"You can check your email," said Grabowski. He sat on the couch and watched her. Through the office door, he could also see the food company employees arrive and take away their tables and chairs.

Finally, Helen turned off her computer. She took two aspirins from her purse and swallowed them.

"I have more questions," Grabowski said, looking at his notes. "Who would want to damage *Musical Chairs*?"

"Many artists were jealous of Soren," said Helen. "He was popular and made a lot of money. But I don't know anyone who would damage his work."

"Who would want to ruin your business by causing the chairs to fall?" continued Grabowski.

Helen laughed. "All owners of art stores want to ruin each others' businesses. But I don't know anyone who would destroy an artist's work."

Grabowski continued: "Louie told me that Lillian and Soren hated each other. But during the show Lillian stayed by Soren at the piano. Why would Lillian stand there?"

Helen raised her eyebrows. "Maybe Lillian knew the rope was going to break! Maybe she wanted to make sure that Soren wouldn't leave until the chairs fell on him!"

"You don't like Lillian, do you?" asked Grabowski.

"No. We used to be friends, but then we went into business together. It ruined our friendship," replied Helen.

"Why?" asked Grabowski.

"Lillian used to be a good artist. But now her work doesn't sell. I need better artists and Lillian doesn't understand that. So we have fights."

"You also had a fight with Soren Berendorf," said Grabowski. "You told him that you would kill him."

Helen put her head in her hands. "Louie always talks too much. Three days before the show Soren told me that he was going to take his collection out."

"Why?" asked Grabowski.

"Soren wanted me to give him more money. I reminded him that he had signed an agreement with me – I would get fifty percent from each work of art of his that I sold. Soren said he would break that agreement. He said he would take his collection back to New York."

"What did you do then?" asked Grabowski.

"I hired guards to stay in the Art Space twenty-four hours a day until the show. I even slept here myself."

"What happens to Soren's collection now?"

Helen shook her head. "I don't know yet. My lawyer thinks that the people who will get Soren's money will keep the agreement. I'll find out tomorrow."

At that moment Lillian and Leo Hochstedder walked in. Lillian's eyes were red. "We came to get the clay heads that people bought yesterday," Lillian said to Helen. "I need to send them to the buyers."

"Bad news," said Helen. "Detective Grabowski says that someone cut the rope holding *Musical Chairs*. That's why they fell."

"Are you sure?" Leo Hochstedder asked Grabowski.

"Positive," said Grabowski. "Someone wanted to break the chairs, or maybe to injure or kill Soren."

Lillian gasped. She put her hands over her mouth.

Grabowski looked at Leo. "The rope was cut with a very sharp knife, near the floor by the food table. Did you see anyone touching the rope there during the evening?"

"Lots of people were near that rope all evening," said Leo. "But I'll bet that Soren cut the rope himself."

"Why would Soren damage his own work?" asked Grabowski, surprised.

"To ruin Helen," said Leo. "He wanted to break his agreement with her and Helen wouldn't let him. Isn't that right, Helen?"

Helen nodded.

"But Soren didn't need to damage his own work to break his agreement," commented Grabowski.

Leo explained: "If Soren broke *Musical Chairs*, Helen couldn't make money from selling it. So she would let him break the agreement. Also, Soren would get the insurance money, and Helen would have to pay him something too.

After such a terrible accident, no good artists would bring their work to the Art Space."

Helen put her head in her hands. "I would be ruined."

Grabowski turned to Lillian. "You stood by Soren and the piano for hours. Why? You hated him, didn't you?"

Lillian bit her fingernails. "These art shows are boring. I didn't want to talk to anyone, so I stood by Soren."

"What did you talk about?" asked Grabowski.

"We didn't talk. Soren played the piano. Louie brought him drinks," said Lillian.

Grabowski said, "Lillian, you weren't at the piano when the chairs fell."

"So?" interrupted her husband, Leo, sharply.

"That was too lucky," answered Grabowski. "Why did you eventually move away from the piano, Lillian?"

Lillian paused. She looked at Louie and at Helen. Then she said, "Louie told me to go upstairs and stand next to my statues because people were asking questions about them."

"No, Lillian," said Helen. "You stepped away from the piano because you cut the rope!"

Lillian jumped to her feet. "I didn't cut it, but I knew the rope was breaking!" she screamed. "I told you, Helen! But you said it was impossible! You cut the rope, Helen! You hated Soren. You said you wanted to kill him! And you did!"

Leo put his arm around his wife. "Calm down, Lillian. Are you sure you knew the rope was breaking? You had a lot to drink last night. Maybe you don't remember well."

Lillian started to cry.

"Sit down, Lillian!" said Grabowski. "Tell me the truth. Did you know that the rope was breaking?"

Lillian sat down on the couch. "Yes. Early in the evening I'd been standing by the food table and I looked down and I saw that the rope was starting to break. I went over to Soren and told him to move away from the piano because the rope was breaking. But he didn't listen to me. So I stayed with him all evening. I thought I could pull him away from the piano if the rope finally broke. But I checked the rope again and I saw it was getting worse. So I went upstairs to tell Helen. She had to stop the show! But Helen wouldn't believe me!" Lillian began crying again.

"Liar!" said Helen.

Grabowski wrote all this into his notebook. "I'll be asking all of you more questions," he said to Lillian, Leo, and Helen. "And I'll be searching everywhere for very sharp knives." He left.

Grabowski drove to the Police Crime Lab on the south side of Milwaukee with the knives from the Art Space and Louie's Antique Shop. To reach the south side, Grabowski drove down 27th Street past the smoking chimneys of the factories of the industrial valley.

The industrial valley divided the north side of Milwaukee from the south. The north side was where people from Germany had settled in the 1850s. Lillian and Leo and Helen lived on the northeast side, near Lake Michigan.

Grabowski owned a little house on the southeast side across the street from a beach on Lake Michigan. People from Poland had settled on the south side of Milwaukee in the early 1900s. There were many Polish churches, schools, clubs, and restaurants. Grabowski's family was Polish. So was Wyoming Syzinski's.

The Police Crime Lab was a one-story brick building inside a high metal fence. Several police cars were parked inside the fence. Grabowski held up his badge to the camera at the gate. The gate opened and Grabowski parked his car inside. He showed his badge to the police guard at the door of the building and the officer opened it.

Another police officer brought out the rope from the Art Space. He showed it to Grabowski. "See? One of the small ropes has very even ends. It was cut with a sharp knife. The other two ropes just broke. Whoever cut the rope pushed the cut ends together. It wasn't obvious at first."

Grabowski handed the officer the knives from Louie's Antique Shop and the Art Space. "If there are any pieces of this rope on these knives, can you match them?"

"If the knives haven't been washed," replied the officer.

***

About that time, Maxine was getting out of a taxi at Mercy Hospital. It was shortly before 3:00 and she had a few minutes before she started work, so she went to the ICU to visit Wyoming. He was still unconscious. Maxine read the notes written by the doctors and nurses. Grabowski had visited him twice that day and so had Wyoming's mother.

Maxine sat down beside Wyoming and held his hand. She knew that even when people are unconscious they can sometimes hear people talking. "You're going to be all right," Maxine told Wyoming. "Soon you will be painting again."

Then she went to visit Rosa Jones. Rosa was almost asleep, but she opened her eyes when Maxine came in. "I'm Dr. Maxine Cassidy," Maxine said. "I knew Latoya."

"Latoya died. Rolondo told me," Rosa said. A tear rolled down her cheek. "Why?"

"She took too much of her TB medicine, I think," said Maxine.

Rosa shook her head. "Latoya didn't have TB."

"Did Latoya have any allergies, like to chocolate? I found a box of chocolates under Latoya's bed," said Maxine. "Where did she get them?"

"Latoya didn't have allergies. She liked chocolates. I don't know where she got them," Rosa whispered. She closed her eyes. Maxine left quietly, leaving Rosa to sleep.

During her evening break Maxine again went upstairs to visit Wyoming. She found Grabowski sitting by his bed. He looked depressed. "I searched Wyoming's apartment today," Grabowski said. "I was trying to find out why he was shot, but I found nothing."

"You don't think it was a gang shooting?" asked Maxine.

Grabowski shook his head. "Rosa told me that she saw the man who shot her, but she didn't recognize him. She didn't recognize the driver of the car either. So she's sure that they aren't from a Milwaukee gang."

"Then who shot Rosa and Wyoming?" asked Maxine.

"I'll find out," said Grabowski with an angry frown. "Wyoming is my friend and I want to know who did this. I'll talk to him when he wakes up."

"If Wyoming wakes up…" Maxine thought to herself. "Have you found out who cut the rope?" she asked.

Grabowski frowned even more. "Helen says that Lillian cut the rope, and Lillian says that Helen did," replied Grabowski. "Soren wanted to ruin Helen, so Helen hated him. And Soren told Lillian she wasn't an artist, so Lillian hated him too. Either of them could have cut that rope!"

Chapter 8   *Officer Koranda*

Grabowski woke early Monday morning feeling tired and depressed. He hadn't slept well. He made a pot of coffee and phoned Mercy Hospital. Wyoming was still unconscious, the nurse reported. Grabowski hung up feeling even more depressed. He took his breakfast outside and sat on the front steps of his little house to eat the scrambled eggs, bacon, toast and coffee.

It was a beautiful morning. The sun was rising and the sweet-smelling air was cool. White birds flew above the blue waters of Lake Michigan and there were a few people walking along the sandy beach. The paper boy rode by on his bicycle and threw Grabowski the morning newspaper.

Grabowski took a drink of his coffee and opened the paper. The front page had another story about the broken chairs and Soren Berendorf. There was a photo of Grabowski himself coming out of the Central Police station. There was also a photo of Louie. Under the photo it read, "The owner of Louie's Antique Shop says the rope was cut so that *Musical Chairs* would fall on Soren Berendorf."

Grabowski threw the paper on the grass. "Louie talks too much," he said to himself. Louie should keep his mouth shut, at least until Grabowski had more information. Grabowski only knew that Lillian and Helen hated Soren Berendorf. Lillian said she knew the rope was breaking during the show. Helen said that Lillian had cut the rope, and Lillian said Helen had cut it. The two women were giving him a headache.

Grabowski had some more coffee and thought about beautiful Helen. She was smart and wore nice perfume. She said that Soren could have ruined her by taking away his collection. Was that true? Helen had divorced a rich doctor. Grabowski wondered how much money she had got in the divorce and how much money she made at the Art Space. Money and crime often went together.

Grabowski finished breakfast and drove to an art store near the Art Space. The owner had been at the show. He was a man in his forties wearing light brown trousers and a green shirt that looked expensive.

"What was your opinion of Soren Berendorf?" asked Grabowski.

"Soren was an extraordinarily talented artist, but I didn't trust him," said the store owner.

"Why not?" asked Grabowski.

"Soren often broke his agreements. Two friends of mine in New York lost a lot of money because Soren took his work out of their stores when he got popular. He sold his work from his home instead, so he got all the money from the sales."

"Agreements are important," agreed Grabowski.

"Especially in the art business," said the man. "For example, I get fifty percent from the sale of an artist's work that I sell in my store. But I work hard for that fifty percent – I find the clients, I pay for the art shows, I pay the taxes. Basically, I pay all the costs of selling a work of art. If artists don't keep their agreements, my business can't stay open."

"Why didn't your friends take Soren to court when he took his work away?" asked Grabowski.

"Lawyers are too expensive," replied the man.

"Did Helen know that Soren had broken these agreements?" asked Grabowski.

The owner of the store nodded. "I told Helen myself when I heard that Soren was bringing *Wood Shapes* to the Art Space. But Helen said that she could force Soren to keep his agreement with her."

"How?" asked Grabowski.

"She didn't say," said the owner. "But Helen is a powerful woman. She built the Art Space into a good business – all by herself. Lillian used to be a good painter, but for the last two years she has only made ugly statues of heads."

"Soren did try to break his agreement with Helen," said Grabowski.

The owner nodded. "I know all about it. Soren came here three days before the show. He wanted to move his collection here. He showed me the agreement he had signed with Helen and asked me to help him break it."

"What did you tell him?" asked Grabowski.

"I told him that Helen was a colleague of mine and I wouldn't do that to her. I told Soren that a smart lawyer might be able to break the agreement. Soren laughed. He said he knew a cheaper way to break his agreement."

"What was he planning to do?" asked Grabowski.

"He didn't tell me," replied the man. "But the next day Helen had guards at the Art Space. They stayed there twenty-four hours a day. Helen was obviously making sure that nothing would go wrong. Helen is desperate for money.

She needs the fifty percent she will get when she sells Soren's *Wood Shapes*."

"Helen isn't rich?" asked Grabowski.

"No. Helen's husband was rich, but when they got divorced, Helen didn't get much. Her husband had a better lawyer than she did. Helen got a few thousand dollars, her clothes, jewelry, and her car. She lost millions of dollars, the big house on Lake Michigan, the boat, the vacation house, and the other two cars."

Grabowski made a note in his notebook, thanked the man and left the store.

At noon, he drove to the Art Space. Helen was in her office talking on the phone and looking at her computer. She was wearing a black suit with a soft purple blouse and a matching handkerchief in the jacket pocket. Her nails were bright red. She was wearing a different perfume. Helen waved hello at Grabowski and said into the phone, "I'll open the Art Space tomorrow for business as usual. You can interview me then." She hung up.

"Newspaper reporter?" asked Grabowski, sitting down on the couch.

Helen smiled. "Yes! Reporters from newspapers, radio, and TV from all over the world are phoning me! They want to know all the details. Do you know who cut the rope yet?"

"Lillian says that you did," said Grabowski.

Helen frowned. "I'll tell you a secret about Lillian: she doesn't see very well. Her sight is bad and getting worse, and she doesn't want anyone to know. She may have seen me checking the rope during the show to make sure it was OK. I wasn't cutting the rope."

"I need to talk to Lillian again soon. I'll go and see her at home," said Grabowski. He made some notes and looked up at Helen again. "Soren wanted to break his agreement with you. How were you planning to stop him?"

But before Helen could answer, the phone rang again. She spoke briefly into the phone, then hung up with a smile. "The owner of an office building in Chicago wants to buy *Musical Chairs!*"

"But it's broken!" said Grabowski, surprised.

"The buyer doesn't care. He says the work is famous," said Helen.

"You'll make a lot of money," said Grabowski.

"Maybe yes; maybe no," replied Helen. "It depends on the people who get Soren's money. Will they keep the agreement he signed?" She looked at her watch. "My lawyer is coming now to advise me. Can you come back at two o'clock? We'll have lunch at the restaurant across the street. I'll turn off my cellphone and you can ask all the questions you want." She turned off her computer.

Grabowski got up to go. "Do you know a man named Wyoming Syzinski? He lives on Fifth Street and Center Street."

Helen thought for a minute. "I don't remember that name. Why?"

"He was supposed to meet me at your show. He's my best friend," said Grabowski.

As Grabowski drove back to the Central Police Station, he thought about the beautiful Helen, and how pleasant it would be to have lunch with her. When he got to the station, the captain of detectives called him into his office.

"What have you got so far on the Soren Berendorf case?" the captain demanded.

"Someone cut the rope holding the chairs, but I don't know who did it. Nobody in Milwaukee liked Soren Berendorf, especially Helen and Lillian, the owners of the Art Space. I found some knives at the Art Space and Louie's Antique Shop and took them to the Crime Lab yesterday. I haven't got the report yet."

The captain said, "While you're waiting for the report, I'm giving you another case. Officer Koranda has disappeared. Find him."

"Koranda? The night guard at the Crime Lab?" asked Grabowski.

"Right. Koranda doesn't answer his home phone or his cellphone."

"Then he's at his fishing cottage," said Grabowski. "He turns off his cellphone when he's fishing."

The captain shook his head. "I called the police in the town near his cottage. No one has seen Koranda there for two weeks. And this morning we found his car parked on Water Street. That's a long way from work or home."

"How long was Koranda's car parked there?" asked Grabowski.

"Two days, probably. Koranda had two days off, then yesterday he didn't come to work. He starts work at eleven o'clock at night."

"Do Koranda's neighbors know where he is?" asked Grabowski.

"Ask them." The captain handed Grabowski a paper with Koranda's address and phone numbers.

"Do you want me to investigate the shooting of Wyoming Syzinski and Rosa Jones?" Grabowski asked.

"No. That was a gang shooting, I'm sure," said the captain. "It was in the inner city and Rosa is the girlfriend of a gang leader. Rolondo's gang and the other gangs keep on shooting each other no matter how many times we put them in jail. Don't waste time on that."

"But Wyoming is my best friend," argued Grabowski.

"Sorry," said the captain. "Wyoming was in the wrong place at the wrong time. Your job is to find Koranda."

Grabowski looked at his watch. It was 12:30. He was having lunch with Helen at 2:00 so he had time to drive to Koranda's house on the west side. He went out to his car. The weather was getting hotter. Grabowski turned on the air conditioner in his car, then took out his handkerchief and wiped the sweat off his forehead.

Officer Koranda lived in a house similar to Maxine's – a two-story building with one apartment on each floor. Koranda lived upstairs. Grabowski rang Koranda's doorbell. No answer. He rang the doorbell of the downstairs apartment. A young woman answered the door. She was holding a baby. Grabowski showed her his police badge.

"Have you seen Officer Koranda recently?" he asked.

"Not for a few days. I thought he'd gone fishing. What's wrong?" asked the woman.

"Officer Koranda has disappeared. Do you have a key to his apartment?"

"Sure. I'll let you inside." She unlocked Koranda's door and followed Grabowski upstairs.

Koranda's apartment didn't have much furniture, just a couch and an armchair in the living room, and a bed in the bedroom. The bedroom closet held two police uniforms and some fishing clothes. Grabowski went into the kitchen. There was a table with two chairs. The refrigerator held eggs and milk.

"Has anyone visited Officer Koranda recently?" Grabowski asked the young woman.

She shook her head. "Officer Koranda hardly ever has visitors. He works nights and comes home about eight o'clock in the morning. He sleeps until late afternoon, then sometimes he cuts the grass or washes his car. Then he sits on the front steps and reads the newspaper. He doesn't go out much. I don't think he has much money. On his days off, he goes fishing and he usually brings me back some fish."

"Does Koranda have any women friends?" asked Grabowski.

The young woman thought. "Several times during the last year a blonde woman has come here. She always waited outside. Each time Koranda gave her a white box – a cooler like the ones he keeps his fish in."

"Can you describe the woman?" asked Grabowski.

"Blonde hair. Tight jeans. Expensive sunglasses."

"Would you recognize her if you saw her again?" asked Grabowski.

"Maybe," answered the woman.

Grabowski found several white coolers in the kitchen. He called the Central Police Station and told them to send fingerprint specialists to test for prints on the coolers. He might be able to find out who Koranda's visitor was. She might know where Koranda was now.

He looked at his watch – already 1:30. He was going to be late for lunch with the beautiful Helen.

Chapter 9 *Man in a box*

Maxine woke up late on Monday. She got the morning paper off the front steps, made coffee and sat on the couch to read it. When she saw the photos of Louie and Grabowski she sighed. Grabowski was probably angry at Louie for telling the newspapers about the rope. Maxine hoped Grabowski wouldn't shout at Louie, because he got upset when people shouted at him. Once Louie had taken a lot of sleeping pills after a fight with a friend.

Maxine went downstairs and knocked on Louie's door. There was no answer. She checked the garage. His car was gone. She telephoned his shop. The phone rang six times. No answer. Maxine got dressed and called a taxi to take her to Louie's Antique Shop.

While she was waiting for the taxi, Maxine called Mercy Hospital Pathology Lab. "Is the autopsy report on Latoya Thompson done? This is Dr. Maxine Cassidy from the ER."

The pathologist replied, "Latoya Thompson took too much INH. Overdose."

"I knew that from the tests done on her stomach in the ER," said Maxine. "Did Latoya have TB?"

"No."

Outside, the taxi driver sounded his horn and Maxine hurried out the door.

When Maxine got out of the taxi in front of Louie's Antique Shop, she spotted Grabowski's little rental car. Was Grabowski inside the shop right now, shouting at Louie?

Maxine hurried over and opened the door. "Louie!" she called.

No answer. Maxine went into the kitchen and opened the door to the garage. Louie's car wasn't there, only Helen's Prius. Maxine returned to the front door. She was just opening it when she saw Grabowski and Helen coming out of the Art Space. Maxine closed the door quickly. She watched them through the window. Helen was wearing a high-fashion black suit and a big black summer hat. Her red lipstick matched her fingernails. Helen locked the door to the Art Space, then she took Grabowski's elbow. Grabowski smiled at her as they crossed the street to a restaurant.

Maxine couldn't believe her eyes. That restaurant was expensive! Why was Helen holding Grabowski's arm? And why was Grabowski smiling? Maxine looked down at her own blue cotton skirt, white blouse, and comfortable shoes. Not high fashion.

Maxine looked at her watch. She still had an hour before she started work at 3:00. She was worried about Louie. Maybe Grabowski had already spoken to Louie and upset him. Louie might have taken some sleeping pills.

Maxine wanted to find him, so she went back into Louie's kitchen and opened the door to the garage. She went down the steps and crossed the garage, passing Helen's Prius. But as she passed the wooden boxes, she paused. One of them was slightly open. She lifted the lid.

Inside the box was a man. He was wrapped in a blanket, showing only his face and neck. He looked dead.

Maxine put her fingers on the man's neck to feel his pulse. His heart was beating, but his skin was very cold.

Maxine reached for her cellphone and called 911. Quickly she described the man's condition and gave the address of Louie's Antique Shop. Then she ran up the stairs, through the shop, out the door, and across the street to the restaurant. Grabowski and Helen were seated at a small table in the corner.

"Grabowski!" Maxine said. "Come over to Louie's Antique Shop! It's urgent!"

"What's wrong?" asked Helen, sharply.

"There's a sick man inside a large wooden box in the garage! I called an ambulance, but you'll have to open the garage door to let it inside," said Maxine.

Helen took out her cellphone. "Let me call Lillian. She might be at the Art Space. She can open the door." She made the call and spoke briefly.

Grabowski stood up. "I looked inside those boxes yesterday. They were empty."

"There's a man inside one now," said Maxine. "Come on, hurry!"

They waited while Helen finished her phone call. Then Grabowski put some money on the table and they hurried out the door. The ambulance was just pulling up. Helen spoke to the driver. She told them to drive around the corner to the entrance to the garage.

Maxine said to Grabowski, "Louie's front door is unlocked, but he isn't here. I went down to the garage to look for him and I saw that the lid to one of those big boxes was slightly open. I lifted the lid and saw the man inside. His heart is beating, but his skin is very cold."

Maxine pushed open the door to Louie's Antique Shop. And there was Louie!

"Where have you been?" shouted Maxine angrily. "I've been searching for you!"

"What's the problem?" asked Louie.

"There's a sick man inside a wooden box in your garage!" said Maxine.

Louie looked at Grabowski and Helen. "But I just drove into the garage," he said, surprised. "I didn't see a man inside any of the wooden boxes!"

Maxine and Grabowski hurried through the kitchen and opened the door to the garage. Louie's green pick-up was now parked next to Helen's Prius. Grabowski went down the stairs. He opened one wooden box. It was empty. He opened the second – also empty. The third box held blankets and one of Lillian's clay heads.

Grabowski looked at Maxine. "Tell me again. Where is this man?"

Chapter 10   *The man disappears*

Helen opened the main garage door. The ambulance was outside. "False alarm," she said to the driver.

Maxine said to Grabowski, "Believe me, I saw a man inside this box."

"Did you turn on the lights when you came down the steps?" Helen asked Maxine.

"No," replied Maxine, "but there was enough light from the kitchen door to see him."

"If you saw him again, would you recognize him?" asked Grabowski.

"Maybe. His face seemed familiar," Maxine replied.

Grabowski frowned at Louie. "You weren't here when Maxine found the man. Did you come back and move him? Where is the man, Louie?"

"I didn't see any man! I went to the corner drugstore to get some more medicine." Louie held out his arms. "See? My arms are still red."

"You drove your car one block?" demanded Grabowski.

"I also drove to a hardware store for knives. You took all my knives," said Louie.

"You left your shop unlocked?" asked Maxine.

"Helen and Lillian were both at the Art Space when I left. They can see from their window when someone comes into my shop. Besides, I was only gone a few minutes," said Louie.

"Louie, you were gone one hour," corrected Maxine, sharply. "I phoned your shop at one thirty and you didn't answer. I came over immediately and you weren't there. Now it's two thirty."

"Where's Lillian?" Grabowski asked Helen. "Didn't you phone her to open the garage door?"

"She didn't answer her phone, so I left a message. Her Lexus is gone – she isn't here."

Louie added, "Her Lexus was here when I left."

"I'm going to talk to Lillian," said Grabowski. "And I'm sending that box to the Police Crime Lab. If a man was inside it, there might be a small piece of his clothing."

Grabowski called the Crime Lab from his cellphone. Then he turned to Louie and Helen.

"Give me your car keys," Grabowski ordered. "I want to search your cars again. I'm also going to search Louie's Antique Shop and the Art Space again. Maxine says there was a man here, and he has to have gone somewhere!"

Helen and Louie handed over their keys. In a few minutes a police officer arrived. Grabowski told him, "Guard these people while I search their shops."

In half an hour Grabowski was back.

"Did you find any men?" Helen joked.

Grabowski shook his head. "I'm going to ask Lillian if she saw someone in the garage – someone who took the man away. Or maybe Lillian took him away herself."

Helen put a hand on Grabowski's arm. "I'm sorry that we had to break off our lunch. Come for dinner at my apartment tonight. You can ask all the questions you want and no one will interrupt." Helen looked at Maxine.

Grabowski also looked at Maxine. "We need to talk, Maxine. I'll drive you to Mercy Hospital."

Grabowski didn't speak until they were a block from the hospital. He pulled over in front of Tony's Fish Fries. "I missed lunch. Let's have some fish fries."

Inside, Maxine ordered fish and a cabbage salad. "I did see a man inside that box," she said to Grabowski.

"I believe you," said Grabowski. "Tell me, why did you hurry down to Louie's shop today?"

"I read in the newspaper that Louie had told a reporter that the rope had been cut. I thought you would get angry with him for giving out police information. Louie gets disturbed when people are angry with him and sometimes he takes too many sleeping pills. "

"Louie said that he had gone to the drugstore for a few minutes, but you couldn't reach him for an hour. I'm sure he's lying," said Grabowski.

Maxine nodded. "Where could Louie have really gone?"

Grabowski said, "There are two possibilities. My colleagues have been investigating Louie for some time. Several antique collectors have told us that his antiques aren't really old. We think that Louie has a secret workshop where his furniture is made to look old, even though it's new."

"I know." Maxine smiled. "Louie told me. He talks a lot. But where else might Louie have gone?"

"I think that Louie saw you find the body. He waited until you had run across the street to get me and Helen. Then he moved it out of the garage," said Grabowski.

Chapter 11   *Lillian is lying*

Grabowski drove to Mercy Hospital, and he and Maxine went to the ICU. Wyoming was still unconscious.

"I told Wyoming a week ago that he could stay at my house as long as he liked," said Grabowski. "If he had stayed, he would be painting – not lying in this hospital."

"Why did he move?" asked Maxine.

"He said that the rooms weren't large enough and the light wasn't good enough for painting," answered Grabowski.

He and Maxine then went to visit Rosa. She was sitting up in bed having lunch.

"Rosa, you were right: Latoya didn't have TB," said Maxine. "So why did she take the INH?"

"I don't know. Please find out, Detective Grabowski," said Rosa. "Whoever gave her the INH should be punished!"

Grabowski and Maxine walked down to the ER together. "I have an idea how Latoya might have taken the INH," said Maxine. "I found a box of chocolates under her bed. We know she ate a lot of them. Rolondo doesn't know where Latoya got the chocolates. Can you take them to the Police Crime Lab and have them tested for INH?"

Grabowski laughed. "INH in chocolates? You can't be serious. Latoya took someone else's INH by mistake. A mistake is not a crime. Police don't investigate mistakes."

Maxine got angry. "If Latoya were rich, the police would investigate how she got the INH. But Latoya was poor, so you won't do anything."

Grabowski sighed. "I'll discuss it with the captain," he said. "But I don't think he will open an investigation. He'll probably say that it was an accident. He won't even let me investigate the shooting of Rosa and Wyoming. He says it's a gang shooting."

"Then I'll find out why Latoya died," said Maxine. "I feel responsible for her death. I should have treated her faster in the ER – and differently." Maxine left without saying goodbye.

Grabowski went out to his car in a bad mood. Maxine was right. Wealthy people got better police protection than poor people. But what could he do? He already had two cases to investigate – to find out why *Musical Chairs* fell on Soren Berendorf, and to find Officer Koranda. Now he also had to find out what happened to the man Maxine had seen in the box in the garage. He needed to speak to Lillian Hochstedder again.

The weather was getting hotter. While he waited for the air conditioner to cool the car, Grabowski telephoned the Crime Lab. "Did any of the knives I sent over have pieces of rope on them?" he asked.

"No. The knives had all been washed."

Another dead end. Grabowski got in the car and drove to the northeast side, near Lake Michigan, to the home of Lillian and Leo Hochstedder. The house was surrounded by a high stone wall with a heavy metal gate. Grabowski pushed a button by the gate and spoke his name into a microphone. The gate opened and he drove inside.

Inside the walls were flower gardens, tall trees, and a swimming pool. Grabowski parked next to Lillian's Lexus. A maid wearing a gray uniform was waiting at the door. She led him to a workshop. Lillian was standing in the doorway wearing jeans and a T-shirt.

"Louie told me you were at the Art Space at around one o'clock today," said Grabowski. "What were you doing?"

"I went there to get some more of the heads that people bought at the show. I'm sending them to the buyers." Lillian pointed at a large wooden box. She started biting her fingernails.

"Helen called your cellphone around two thirty," said Grabowski. "You didn't answer. Where were you?"

"I was at home at two thirty. I didn't hear my cellphone."

"Can I look around your workshop?" asked Grabowski.

"Look wherever you want," said Lillian. She was still biting her nails.

Grabowski walked around the room and saw paints, brushes, and clay. There was a workbench with a lot of drawers, but he found only more brushes and paints in them. Standing near the door were two large wooden boxes, like those in the garage at the Art Space. They were nailed shut. "Please open these boxes," Grabowski said to Lillian.

"Why?" she demanded.

"Just open them," Grabowski answered. But when Lillian opened the boxes, he found only two clay heads inside each one.

In the middle of the room was a platform with a cloth over it. Grabowski lifted the cloth. An unfinished clay head sat on the platform. One eye had a glass ball in it, but the other was empty. The teeth looked real. Lillian took the cloth from Grabowski and put it back over the head.

Grabowski left without asking any more questions. But as he drove out the gate, he felt that he had missed something important.

Chapter 12 *Wyoming wakes up*

The ER was busy Monday afternoon. At 8:00 that evening an ICU nurse called Maxine to say that Wyoming Syzinski was awake. It was quieter by then, so Maxine hurried upstairs. She leaned over his bed and held his hand. "Hello, Wyoming, I'm Maxine," she said quietly.

Wyoming smiled. "Grabowski's Maxine?"

She nodded. Wyoming had very blue eyes, Maxine noticed. "How are you feeling?"

"Glad I'm alive," said Wyoming.

"I'll tell Grabowski and your mother that you're awake. Grabowski is trying to find out who shot you."

"I can't remember a thing." Wyoming closed his eyes.

Maxine then went into Rosa's room. The young woman was sitting up in bed painting her fingernails purple. She was wearing a pink nightdress. "Hi, Doc!" she called cheerfully.

"Wyoming woke up," said Maxine. "He's going to be all right."

"I'll visit him when my fingernails dry." Rosa smiled. "Wyoming's a great artist. He drew a picture of me and it looks just like me!"

"Can you describe the person who shot you and the driver of the car?" asked Maxine. "When Wyoming feels stronger, he could draw the people, and that might help Detective Grabowski find them."

Maxine knew that Grabowski's captain hadn't allowed Grabowski to investigate the shooting. But maybe a drawing of the gunman would change his mind.

Back in the ER, Maxine found a note from Shirley. Grabowski had called. He said that his captain would not open an investigation to find out how Latoya got the INH.

Maxine called Grabowski back immediately. But he didn't answer his work or home phones, or his cellphone. She left messages about Wyoming and banged down the telephone.

"Take it easy," said Shirley. "Grabowski's working."

"No, he's having dinner with Helen Mueller and he's switched his phone off," said Maxine. "I interrupted his lunch date so she invited him for dinner. Grabowski has a date with Helen!"

Shirley raised her eyebrows. "And you say you're not in love?"

At 8:30 Rolondo came into the ER carrying a suitcase. "I'm bringing Rosa some more clothes," he said.

"Can you give me a ride home tonight?" Maxine asked.

"This is the last time," said Rolondo. "Tomorrow I'll help you buy a new car. Did you find out where Latoya got the TB medicine?"

"Grabowski thinks that Latoya took someone else's medicine by accident," Maxine said.

"Keep looking and find out why Latoya died. And do it soon. I don't want Rosa and me to die of the same thing," said Rolondo.

At midnight Rolondo came to take Maxine home.

"Can we go to Wyoming's apartment before you take me home?" Maxine asked Rolondo. "I want to get some drawing paper and pencils for him. Rosa can describe the people she saw in the car to Wyoming, and he can draw a picture. Grabowski can show the picture to people around Milwaukee. Someone might recognize them."

"I'll want to see those pictures myself," said Rolondo.

Rolondo drove Maxine to Wyoming's apartment. He opened the door with his knife and turned on the light. Rolondo and Maxine stared in surprise. Wyoming's books, papers, and clothing were spread around the room and all over the floor.

"Grabowski did this. I saw him come here yesterday," Rolondo said. "He should be more careful when he's searching people's things. Get your paper and pencils while I go to Rosa's apartment. Now she wants red fingernail polish." Rolondo went out to the hall and closed the door.

Maxine found several notebooks and pencils then heard a noise in the bedroom. "Who's there?" she called. There was no answer. Probably a rat, she decided. She walked into the bedroom to look for paints. Then something hit her on the head and everything went dark.

Chapter 13   *Helen knows something*

When Maxine woke up, Rolondo was putting a wet cloth on her head. He looked worried. "Somebody must have hit you."

Maxine groaned. "Did you see the person?"

"No. I called Grabowski. He'll be here soon and he's really angry that you came here tonight. He's also angry at me for bringing you." Rolondo looked out the window. "Grabowski's here; I'm leaving." Rolondo hurried out the door.

A few moments later Grabowski ran into the room. "Are you crazy?" he shouted at Maxine. "I told you not to come to this area at night! I'm taking you to the ER!"

"Home. Please," said Maxine.

Grabowski looked around at the papers and clothing, spread over the floor. "Rolondo did this! I'm putting him under arrest!"

"We thought you made this mess when you searched the apartment." Maxine held her head. It hurt when she talked.

Grabowski shook his head. "Whoever hit you searched the apartment. But what was the person looking for? There's nothing here but art supplies and Wyoming's clothes."

Grabowski drove Maxine home. She got into bed while he put ice into a bag. Grabowski put the bag on Maxine's head, then pulled up a chair and sat down. "Why were you in Wyoming's apartment?"

"I wanted art paper and pencils for him," said Maxine. "Rosa can describe the driver of the car and the person who shot them. Wyoming could draw their pictures."

"Why didn't you call me? I could have got the art paper," said Grabowski.

"I did call you. You didn't answer," replied Maxine.

Grabowski didn't say anything for a minute. "I was having dinner with Helen," he said finally.

"You had a date with Helen, you mean," said Maxine.

"It wasn't a date," said Grabowski. "I think Helen knows who cut the rope. I wanted to get her to talk. I thought she might say something that would help me figure out what's going on."

"What did you find out?" asked Maxine.

"Not much. But I think Helen knows all about the man you saw in the wooden box," said Grabowski.

Chapter 14   *Wyoming draws*

Tuesday morning, Maxine woke up at 11:00. Her headache was gone. She got the newspaper from the front steps and read it while she ate breakfast. According to the paper, Grabowski still didn't know why *Musical Chairs* had fallen on Soren Berendorf.

"And I still don't know how Latoya got the INH," Maxine thought. She phoned the Wisconsin State Laboratory in Madison. A friend of hers worked there; maybe he could help.

"Ivan!" Maxine said when her friend answered the phone. "Can you do a lab test for me? A young woman named Latoya died of an INH overdose. The hospital tests showed that there was also chocolate in her stomach. I have three chocolates that I found in her apartment. I think the chocolates may have INH in them. Can you test them for me?"

"Why don't you ask the police to send them to the Police Crime Lab?" suggested Ivan.

"Because the police won't open an investigation," replied Maxine.

"Why do you think there was INH in these chocolates?" asked Ivan.

"Latoya didn't have TB. She got sick suddenly at home. These chocolates are my only clue."

"OK," said Ivan. "Send them today. I may have some results tomorrow."

Now Maxine had to get the chocolates to Madison, a city two hours away by car. She called Rolondo on his cellphone.

"Remember that box of chocolates I found in Latoya's bedroom? Can you take it to a lab in Madison today? A friend of mine there will test the chocolates. If he finds INH in them, then we'll know how Latoya got the INH."

"I'll come right over," Rolondo said. "But before I go to Madison, I'm taking you to buy a car. My cousin sells cars. You can pay him when you get your insurance money."

By 2:00 Maxine had bought a car from Rolondo's cousin. It was a used blue Ford Taurus X, but it looked like new. She drove to Mercy Hospital and had enough time before work to visit Wyoming. He was out of the ICU and in a room near Rosa. A nurse had combed his hair and given him a shave.

"You look better," said Maxine.

"That's what Grabowski said this morning," said Wyoming. "He brought me the art paper, notebooks, and pencils you got from my apartment."

"Can you draw the person who shot you?" said Maxine. "Rosa says she can describe the people in the car."

"I'll try," said Wyoming.

Maxine picked up one of the art notebooks on the bed and looked through the pages. Suddenly she gasped. "This is a drawing of Lillian Hochstedder! How do you know her?"

"Lillian came out to Arizona a year ago. She was a student in an art class that I was teaching."

"Did you see Lillian when you came back to Milwaukee?" asked Maxine.

Wyoming nodded. "Yes. I went to her house and I saw her statues." He frowned. "They're terrible and I told her to stop making them. I'm sorry I said that, because Lillian got very upset. Helen Mueller walked in then. She told me about Soren Berendorf's show at the Art Space. I hadn't seen Soren in twenty years, so I wanted to see his work."

"Did you know Soren well?" Maxine asked.

Wyoming nodded. "Yes. We grew up together, although we were never close friends. Helen gave me an invitation and called me the afternoon before the show to remind me. But shortly after she called, I got shot."

At that moment Grabowski walked in. Maxine pointed at Wyoming's drawing. "Wyoming knows Lillian. She was a student of his in Arizona. Wyoming went to her house to see her statues. Helen was there too, and she invited him to the show."

Grabowski frowned. "Helen told me that she didn't remember any Wyoming Syzinski."

"Wyoming Syzinski is a hard name to forget!" commented Maxine.

Wyoming said, "I'm sorry I missed the art show. I'll call Soren today and tell him I'll see *Wood Shapes* when I get out of the hospital. I especially want to see *Musical Chairs*."

Grabowski shook his head. "I'm sorry to tell you this, but Soren is dead."

"Dead? How?" Wyoming's face went white.

"At the show, the rope holding up *Musical Chairs* broke and the chairs fell on Soren," said Grabowski.

"The rope broke? How could that happen?" Wyoming was amazed.

"Someone cut the rope," Grabowski explained. "I haven't found out who or why. Do you know anyone who might have wanted to damage Soren's art or injure Soren?"

Wyoming shook his head. "No, although twenty years ago most of my friends in Milwaukee didn't like him. Soren thought he was better than the rest of us."

Maxine answered her cellphone. It was Shirley in the ER. "Where are you?" Shirley demanded. "A lot of sick people are waiting for you!" Maxine hurried back to the ER.

At 8:00 that evening Maxine went back to see Wyoming. Rosa was sitting on his bed dressed in a red nightdress that matched her fingernails. She was describing the man who shot her, and Wyoming was drawing in his notebook.

When Wyoming saw Maxine, he put down his pencil. "Rosa can describe the man who shot us, but when I draw I feel anxious and can't concentrate. I keep hearing the car and the gunshots."

"Then you should rest," said Maxine.

"Maybe Latoya saw the person," suggested Wyoming. "Maybe she looked out of the window when she heard the shots. She could help Rosa describe the people to another artist."

Rosa started to cry. "Latoya got sick that same night. She died here in the hospital."

"Died!" said Wyoming. "But Latoya was in my apartment at lunch. She wasn't sick at all. She ate nearly all my chocolates! And she took the rest with her!"

"Were they in a big red box?" asked Maxine.

"That's right." Wyoming nodded.

At midnight, after work, Maxine went upstairs to visit Wyoming again. Drawings were spread over his bed. "I finished drawing the man who shot us and the driver of the car," Wyoming said.

"Could you draw another man if I describe him?" asked Maxine.

"I'll try." Wyoming picked up his pencil.

Maxine closed her eyes and tried to remember the man inside the wooden box in the garage of the Art Space. "He had a long nose, lots of dark hair, and big ears that stuck out," she began.

She gave Wyoming more details as he drew. She watched the man's face appear on the page. Suddenly she gasped. "I've seen this man before! He was at the Art Space during the show. I remember his big ears. He was upstairs talking to Leo Hochstedder!"

Just then Grabowski walked in. He picked up Wyoming's drawings from the bed.

"Those are drawings of the man who shot me and the driver of the car," Wyoming explained.

"I'm not supposed to investigate the shooting, but when I'm off duty tonight I can show these to people in the bars downtown," said Grabowski. "Someone might recognize the men."

Maxine handed Grabowski the drawing that Wyoming had just finished. "This is the man I saw inside the wooden box. I've seen him before, Grabowski! He was at the Art Space, talking to Leo Hochstedder."

Grabowski stared at the drawing. He sat down. "That's Officer Koranda!" he said. "Koranda disappeared four days ago. I've been searching for him!" He took out his cellphone and called his captain.

"Koranda was seen inside a wooden box in the Art Space yesterday," Grabowski said into his phone. "He was unconscious. A person who saw Koranda alive at the Art Space on Saturday night just identified him from a drawing. But Koranda disappeared again and I don't know where he is."

"Find him," ordered the captain. "Do you need support?"

"Not yet," said Grabowski. He closed his cellphone.

Maxine was puzzled. "Why would a police officer be unconscious inside a box in Louie's garage? And where is he now?"

Grabowski frowned. "Lillian, Helen, and Louie must know more than they are telling me. I'm going to get some answers!"

Chapter 15 *More questions for Lillian*

At 8:00 the next morning Grabowski finished breakfast and took a walk down by Lake Michigan. The air by the lake was cool and smelled slightly of fish. Grabowski yawned. He was tired. After he had left Mercy Hospital the previous night he had gone to a number of bars in the inner city to show people Wyoming's drawings. He was off duty and was investigating the shooting on his own time. No one he'd spoken to had recognized the people in the drawings. Then Grabowski had gone to Rolondo's apartment, where the gang leader had been playing cards with four other men. None of them had recognized anyone in the drawings either.

Grabowski had gone home to bed at 3:00 am exhausted. But he couldn't sleep. Rolondo knew everyone involved in crime in the inner city. So if he and his friends didn't recognize the people in the drawings, who had shot Wyoming and Rosa? And why?

After his walk, Grabowski drove over to Koranda's house and rang the doorbell of the downstairs apartment. The young woman answered the door. He showed her Wyoming's drawing of Lillian. "Is this the woman who visited Officer Koranda?" he asked.

The young woman looked carefully at the drawing. She nodded. "That's her. She came here a few times."

"And each time she came, did Koranda give her a white box?"

"Yes." The woman nodded. "Is Officer Koranda coming home again?"

"I hope so," said Grabowski.

Grabowski got back in his car and called Louie on his cellphone. Grabowski wanted to show him the drawing of Koranda. Maybe Louie had talked to Koranda at the art show. But Louie didn't answer his home phone, his cellphone or the telephone at Louie's Antique Shop.

Grabowski then called Lillian. "I have a drawing to show you," he said. "And I have more questions."

"I'm calling my lawyer," Lillian said.

"Good idea," said Grabowski. "You and your lawyer can talk to me at the Central Police Station."

"OK." Lillian sighed. "I won't call my lawyer. Come over to my house. We'll talk here."

Grabowski drove back toward Lake Michigan. As he got near to Lillian's house, he opened the car window. The air was cooler near the lake and smelled of grass, trees, and flowers. Not only did rich people have nicer houses and cars, but also they had nicer weather, Grabowski thought. He parked next to the Lexus in front of the house.

Lillian was waiting at the front door. She had dark shadows under her eyes. She led Grabowski to a room overlooking the swimming pool. Grabowski sat on a couch with soft cushions. The maid brought him some iced tea.

Grabowski held up Wyoming's drawing. "Do you know this man?" he asked. "His name is Officer Koranda. He's a guard at the Police Crime Lab."

"No," said Lillian. "I don't know him."

"I think you do," said Grabowski. He held up the drawing that Wyoming had done of her. "Officer Koranda's neighbor recognized you from this drawing. She said you came to Koranda's house several times. Each time you came, Koranda gave you a large white box – like the coolers he puts his fish in."

Lillian put her head in her hands. "OK, I did go to Koranda's house. And he did give me the coolers."

"What was inside these coolers?" demanded Grabowski.

"Art supplies," replied Lillian.

Grabowski frowned. "Art supplies in coolers? Why would Officer Koranda give you art supplies?"

Lillian didn't answer.

"Lillian," said Grabowski, "answer my questions. You're involved in a possible murder investigation."

"Murder?" Lillian's face went white. "But Officer Koranda isn't dead!"

"How do you know? Koranda disappeared four days ago. He was seen unconscious inside a wooden box in the garage at the Art Space. He could be dead."

"No! That's impossible!" shouted Lillian.

"Then where is Officer Koranda, Lillian?" demanded Grabowski.

She started to cry.

Grabowski sat down and took out his notebook. "Let's start again. This time tell me the truth. What was inside the white coolers that Koranda gave you?"

Lillian put her hands over her face. "Bones," she whispered.

Grabowski couldn't believe his ears. "Bones? I don't understand."

"Human heads. Skulls. I bought them from Officer Koranda. He said it was OK, that it was legal. He told me the skulls were from people who had died a long time ago and nobody knew who they were."

Grabowski was thinking. Officer Koranda worked at the Police Crime Lab. The Crime Lab was where people brought any bones found in Milwaukee. If the bones were human, the police at the Crime Lab tried to identify them. If they couldn't identify the bones, they were buried in the cemetery. But Koranda must have sold some of the skulls to Lillian.

"Why did you buy these skulls?" Grabowski asked.

"I copied them to make my clay heads," said Lillian.

Grabowski thought that sounded like the truth. But why were Lillian's hands shaking so much? "What did you do with the skulls when you were through copying them?" he asked.

"I gave them back to Officer Koranda," said Lillian.

"How did you know that you could buy human skulls from Koranda?" Grabowski asked.

"When my husband, Leo, was a university student, he got bones from the Police Crime Lab. He used the bones to help him study the human body." Lillian tried to light a cigarette, but her hands were shaking too much.

"Take me to your workshop," said Grabowski. "I want to see some skulls."

Lillian dropped her cigarette. "I don't have any left."

"Show me your workshop, anyway," said Grabowski.

Lillian led Grabowski to her workshop and watched him look around. The wooden boxes were gone, but there were two unfinished clay heads on tall platforms. Wet cloths were over each head. Grabowski lifted the cloth from one. The clay was very thick. Two straws came out of the nose. There was a hole for the mouth.

"I just started making that head," said Lillian. She put the cloth back over it.

Grabowski opened all the cupboards, but he found nothing interesting.

"Yesterday Louie told me that he saw your Lexus at the Art Space at one o'clock," Grabowski said. "Shortly after that, Officer Koranda was found inside a wooden box in the garage. Did you see those boxes?"

Lillian put her hands over her face.

"Answer me, Lillian," said Grabowski. "Did you see anyone else come into the garage?"

"No!" whispered Lillian.

"After that you drove your Lexus out of the garage. Then Helen phoned you, but you didn't answer your cellphone. Where were you, Lillian?"

"I was here," said Lillian, biting her nails.

Grabowski was getting angry. "I want to see your car."

Lillian and Grabowski walked out to the Lexus. She opened the doors and Grabowski looked inside. "You just cleaned your car, inside and out, didn't you?" he asked.

Lillian nodded.

Grabowski got in his car and watched Lillian walk into the house. He was getting nowhere. He tried Louie again, but he still didn't answer any of his numbers.

Grabowski then called the captain of detectives. "Koranda sold human skulls from the Crime Lab to Lillian Hochstedder," he reported. "She says she copied them for her clay statues of heads. Lillian was in the garage of the Art Space before Koranda was found there, but she says that she doesn't know anything about him or the box."

"Do you believe her?" asked the captain.

"I don't believe anyone in this case," said Grabowski. "I need some search orders. I want to get into the computer at the Art Space. And I want to search the Hochstedders' house and Leo's medical office. I think that everyone in this case knows more than they're telling me."

Chapter 16   *Sleeping pills*

At 10:00 Wednesday morning Maxine was sleeping when her phone rang. Her friend Ivan was calling from the Wisconsin State Laboratory in Madison. "I have the results on those chocolates," Ivan said. "You were right. There was INH in all three."

"Now I have to find out who put it there," said Maxine.

She hung up, then her cellphone rang. It was Grabowski. Maxine gave him the news about the chocolates.

"And how did the INH get inside the chocolates?" Grabowski asked.

"I don't know yet," admitted Maxine. "What have you discovered about the rope?"

"Nothing new yet, but I've learned that Lillian Hochstedder was buying skulls from Officer Koranda," replied Grabowski.

"Skulls?" asked Maxine.

"Human skulls. When human bones are found around Milwaukee they're brought to the Police Crime Lab and we try to identify them. Koranda sold some skulls to Lillian and she copied them to make her clay heads."

"Isn't it against the law to buy and sell human skulls?" Maxine asked.

"Koranda shouldn't have done it. Human bones should be buried. Now I'm trying to find Louie. I want him to tell me exactly what Helen, Lillian, Leo, and Soren did after they hung *Musical Chairs*. Louie doesn't answer any of his phones. Do you know where he is?"

"Maybe he's asleep," said Maxine. "I'll wake him up. Stay on the line."

Maxine took her cellphone downstairs to Louie's apartment and knocked on the door. "Louie!" she shouted. No answer. Maxine went down and looked in the garage. Louie's car was there. Alarmed, she ran upstairs for her key to Louie's apartment and unlocked his door. He was lying on the bathroom floor.

"Louie!" Maxine shouted. She shook his arm, then felt for a pulse. His heartbeat was slow and weak, and he was breathing very slowly. She spoke into the phone. "Grabowski, I'm calling 911! Louie's unconscious. I don't know what's wrong with him."

The ambulance arrived quickly. The EMTs got Louie inside the ambulance and put him on the breathing machine. "Take him to Mercy ER," ordered Maxine. She picked up Louie's keys from his table and followed the ambulance in her new Ford Taurus X.

When she got to Mercy Hospital, the ER doctor and nurse on duty were pumping everything out of Louie's stomach. The doctor put some of it into a small bottle to send to the lab to find out what Louie had eaten.

"I'll take it," offered Maxine. She hurried to the lab and waited for the results.

"Sleeping pills," said the technician, picking up the phone to call the ER doctor.

Maxine went back to the ER. "How's Louie?" she asked the doctor.

"He's conscious now, but he's very weak and having trouble breathing. He'll stay in the hospital overnight."

A nurse took Louie to a room; Maxine followed and sat down by his bed. "Louie, the man I saw inside the box in the garage was a police officer named Koranda. You must help Grabowski find him, or you will be in serious trouble. Where were you when I found Officer Koranda?"

Louie spoke quietly. "When I got to my shop that day, Helen was in the kitchen. She has a key to the shop from the garage. She told me that someone had called from my workshop in south Milwaukee. The person wanted me to come right away."

"The workshop where people make furniture for you that looks like antiques?"

"Don't tell Grabowski!" said Louie.

"I won't," said Maxine. She decided not to tell Louie that Grabowski already knew about the workshop. "When you got to your workshop, what was the problem?"

"There was no problem. They hadn't called me. Helen had made a mistake," Louie replied.

"What pills did you take this morning?" Maxine asked next.

"The pills you recommended to stop my skin itching," replied Louie. "I took three of them, then I took six more. I know that was too many, but I was really itching!"

"But the ER doctor found sleeping pills in your stomach," Maxine said.

Louie looked confused. "Sleeping pills? No!"

"Where did you get the allergy pills? Could anyone have touched them?" asked Maxine.

"I got them at the drugstore. I take them with me when I go to my shop because I need them during the day.

Yesterday I put them in the kitchen, and then I brought them home after work."

"Louie, I think this may have something to do with *Musical Chairs* falling on Soren Berendorf at the art show. Tell me everything you can remember about that evening – what everyone did before the rope broke, starting from when you all hung the chairs over the piano. Every detail, Louie!"

Louie nodded. "At five o'clock we all helped Soren hang the chairs over the piano. Then we went home and changed clothes for the show. We all came back just before eight o'clock. The food company brought the food then, and we helped carry it in."

"Who helped with the food?" asked Maxine.

Louie counted on his fingers. "Me, Helen, Lillian, and Leo. Soren didn't help. Then we all checked the rope to make sure it was tied tightly to the hook on the floor. So I know that the rope was OK just before the show."

"When did you notice that the rope was breaking?" asked Maxine.

"After midnight. I was standing by the food table and I looked down at the rope near the hook on the floor. Two of the three smaller ropes had broken! I couldn't believe my eyes! *Musical Chairs* could fall on Soren and Lillian! I hurried over right away and told them to get away from the piano! I said the rope was breaking! But Soren laughed. He said I was joking. And Lillian wouldn't leave Soren."

Maxine said, "So you told Lillian that she should be near her statues to answer questions about them."

Louie nodded. "It was a way to get her away from the piano. But then Lillian decided she needed to talk to

Helen and came upstairs with me. When we got upstairs, I told Helen that the rope was breaking. I told her to come downstairs. But Helen didn't believe me either! She said it was impossible. So I decided to tell Grabowski. But the rope broke before I could get to him."

"Why do you think Helen said it was impossible?" asked Maxine.

"Maybe Helen cut the rope," said Louie. "Maybe she wanted *Musical Chairs* to break. Helen really hated Soren. He wanted to ruin her by breaking his agreement."

"After the chairs fell, why didn't you tell Grabowski that you knew the rope had been breaking?" asked Maxine.

"Helen told me not to say anything," said Louie. "She said we would get into a lot of trouble."

At that moment Louie's cellphone rang. Maxine picked it up and looked at the caller ID. It was Helen. Maxine answered the phone. "Dr. Maxine Cassidy speaking."

"Where's Louie?" demanded Helen.

"In the hospital," said Maxine.

Helen gasped. "Did Louie take too many sleeping pills? Is he dead?"

"Louie will be fine. How did you know he took sleeping pills?" asked Maxine.

"Louie takes sleeping pills when he's upset, and he's very upset now. Detective Grabowski found out that Louie cut the rope. He's going to arrest him."

Maxine went out into the hall so she could talk to Helen without Louie hearing. "Why does Grabowski think Louie cut the rope?" Maxine asked.

"I told him," replied Helen. "I saw Louie cut the rope right before the show. He used a knife from his kitchen."

"Why would Louie cut the rope?" Maxine asked.

"Louie was very angry at Soren. Soren had found out that many of Louie's antiques aren't old, and he was going to tell the police."

"An interesting theory, but I don't believe a word of it," said Maxine. She hung up and phoned Grabowski. "Do you think Louie cut the rope?" she demanded. "Are you going to arrest him?"

Grabowski sighed. "No, I'm not going to arrest Louie. Helen told me that Louie cut it, but I think she's lying."

"Louie is in Mercy Hospital," said Maxine. "He took too many sleeping pills. He says he only took his allergy pills, and also that he knew the rope was breaking. He told Lillian, Soren, and Helen about it, but they wouldn't believe him. Louie says he was going to tell you, but the rope broke before he could get to you."

"Do you think that one of them gave him sleeping pills so that he couldn't tell me this now?" asked Grabowski.

"It could be," said Maxine.

"Well, it wasn't Lillian," said Grabowski. "Lillian told me that she saw that the rope was breaking early in the evening. She said she warned Soren, but he didn't believe her. That's why Lillian wouldn't leave the piano. She was trying to protect Soren."

Maxine thought about Helen and Soren, about Lillian and her husband, Dr. Leo Hochstedder, about Louie, and about Wyoming. "First Latoya was poisoned with INH, next Wyoming and Rosa were shot, and finally *Musical Chairs* fell on Soren," she said. "It happened in that order, and it happened that way for a reason."

"And now someone gave Louie sleeping pills," added Grabowski.

"Louie told me that he watched everyone check the rope just before the show," remembered Maxine. "One of those people cut the rope. That person knows Louie was watching."

"But which person?" said Grabowski. "Helen, Lillian, Soren himself, or Leo? Or Louie could be lying. He could have cut it himself. I'm coming to the hospital to talk to him. Maybe he can remember more details about that evening."

"And I want to ask Wyoming where he got those chocolates," said Maxine. "I also want to know more about Lillian's statues."

"Don't bother," said Grabowski. "They're just clay heads."

Maxine closed the cellphone, went back to Louie's room and returned it to him. She said goodbye and then she went to Wyoming's room.

"Where did you get that box of chocolates?" she asked.

"From Lillian," Wyoming replied. "The morning of the art show she came to my apartment to see my work. The chocolates were a gift for my new apartment."

Chapter 17 *Skulls!*

At midnight, after work, Maxine drove to Louie's Antique Shop and parked in front. She had brought with her all of Louie's keys. She unlocked the door of the shop and stepped inside. Then she paused. Maybe she should call Grabowski to tell him what she was planning, she thought. No, she decided. She needed to know more about Lillian's statues. Then she would know who had cut the rope, who had poisoned Latoya, and who had shot Wyoming and Rosa. And she would know why. Then she would call Grabowski.

Maxine went into the kitchen and opened the door to the garage. She turned on the light and went down the steps. Two big wooden boxes were still there. She lifted the lids. Empty.

She went up the stairs to the Art Space. She unlocked the door with Louie's key, went through the office and upstairs to the room where Lillian's clay heads were. She turned on the light. The glass eyes in the statues seemed to move.

Maxine took a deep breath. Then she picked up one of the clay heads, lifted it over her head, and threw it on the floor. The head cracked, but it didn't break. A glass eye fell out. She picked the head up again, lifted it over her head, and threw it down again. This time the clay broke apart. In front of Maxine was a human skull.

"So you found out my secret," said a voice behind her.

Maxine turned around. Lillian was standing in the doorway.

"I wanted to be sure," said Maxine. "I thought there were real skulls under the clay, but I needed to make sure."

"You are like all doctors. You need to make sure. So you do more tests and more tests. Even though you can't help me."

"You're talking about your eyes, aren't you?" asked Maxine.

"Eye. One eye. About two years ago I woke up one morning and I couldn't see out of one eye. There was light, but nothing else. The eye specialist said, 'There's bleeding inside your eye. But I have to do some tests to make sure.' I spent thousands of dollars on tests by eye specialists. They all said, 'You have bleeding inside your eye, but there's nothing we can do. We can't save your eye.'"

"I thought you had trouble with your sight," said Maxine. "At the art show you put your glass down on the piano, but it was too close to the edge and it fell off."

"I can't judge distance because I have sight in only one eye. An artist who can't judge distance can't paint pictures. I tried to paint using only one eye, but I couldn't. So I went to Arizona and took a class with Wyoming. He tried to teach me how to judge distance using only one eye. But I couldn't do it. I couldn't even make statues out of clay."

Maxine asked, "That's when you started making statues by putting clay over real skulls?"

Lillian laughed. "Yes. Officer Koranda sold me a skull and I put clay over it, with glass for eyes. It was easy! Nobody knew that it was a real human head. It sold right away! So I asked Koranda for more skulls and I went to his apartment to collect them. My clay heads became popular! Officer Koranda kept selling me more skulls."

"Then Soren Berendorf found out," said Maxine.

Lillian stopped laughing. "Helen brought Soren to my workshop. One of my heads wasn't finished. Soren had a knife. Before I could stop him, he cut off some of the clay and saw the skull underneath. So did Helen." Lillian sat down on the floor. She put her head in her hands.

"What happened then?" asked Maxine quietly.

"Helen laughed. But Soren was angry; he said I wasn't a real artist. He said he refused to be in a show with me. He told Helen he was going to take his collection back to New York, where there are real artists."

"What did Helen say?" asked Maxine.

"Helen reminded Soren that he had signed an agreement with her to keep *Wood Shapes* at the Art Space for one year. Soren said he would break the agreement. He said if Helen tried to stop him, he would cut open my heads at the show. All the newspaper reporters in Milwaukee would see. Everyone would know there were human skulls inside. I would be ruined and so would Helen. Everyone would know that the Art Space didn't have real artists."

"So you decided to stop Soren from opening your statues," said Maxine. "You cut the rope holding up *Musical Chairs* so that it would fall on him. Helen could close the show immediately and the newspapers would never find out about the skulls."

"No," said Lillian. "I hated Soren, but I didn't cut that rope! When I saw the rope was breaking I warned Soren and Helen. But they wouldn't believe me. I told Grabowski all this."

"Let's talk about Wyoming," said Maxine. "He came to your house, didn't he?"

"Yes. Wyoming saw my statues. He told me that they weren't real art and that I should stop making them. Helen was there too. She told Wyoming about our show and he said that he had known Soren for twenty years. So Helen invited him."

"The morning before the art show, you went to Wyoming's apartment, didn't you?"

"Yes. I wanted to see his work," said Lillian.

"You brought Wyoming chocolates. Chocolates with INH in them."

"What's INH?" asked Lillian. "Anyway, the chocolates weren't from me. Helen gave me the chocolates. Helen told me to give them to Wyoming. She said they were a gift for his new apartment."

"One more question," said Maxine. "Where is Officer Koranda?"

"Stop talking to her, Lillian," said a voice at the door. Leo Hochstedder was in the doorway.

Chapter 18   *Leo and Lillian tell all*

Leo Hochstedder stepped into the room. "I told Lillian not to buy skulls from Koranda. I told her not to put them inside her clay heads. Some of my colleagues bought Lillian's statues! What if they found out there are human skulls inside? My colleagues would stop working with me! But no one knows. Maxine, you won't tell our colleagues, will you?" Leo's hands were shaking.

Maxine shook her head. "No."

"Let's go home, Lillian," said Leo.

"Wait!" called Maxine, but Leo and Lillian went quickly down the stairs, through the office, and down to the garage. Maxine hurried after them. Lillian got into their Lexus and Leo went to open the garage door. Quickly, Maxine went to the back of their car and opened the trunk. Inside was Officer Koranda. His eyes were closed. Maxine put her fingers on Koranda's neck to feel his pulse. His heart was beating and he was breathing. Maxine shook his shoulder. "Koranda!" she said loudly, but he didn't answer.

Maxine pulled out her cellphone.

"Wait!" said Leo. "He'll wake up soon. We'll take him home. He'll be fine."

"Leo," said Maxine, "we need to call an ambulance."

Lillian started to cry. "We're in a lot of trouble! Please help us! No one must know about this."

Maxine looked at Leo. "Koranda was at the art show. I saw him looking at Lillian's clay heads. I saw you talking to him. Then I saw you both go downstairs together."

Leo nodded. "We went to the garage. Koranda wanted a lot of money. He said he would tell the reporters that there were real skulls inside Lillian's clay heads. We had a fight. Koranda fell down and hit his head."

"So you hid him," said Maxine.

Leo nodded. "I heard *Musical Chairs* fall. I knew the police would come and that if they found him, Koranda would tell them everything. So I put him in the trunk of our car."

"Where did you take him?" asked Maxine.

"We locked him inside our basement. He had plenty of food and water, but he didn't know where he was. Then we asked Helen what to do. She told us he wasn't safe there. Detective Grabowski said he was going to search everywhere he could think of for sharp knives. Helen thought he would search our houses. She told us to pay Koranda the money he wanted. Then we should give him drugs to make him sleep and bring him to the garage at the Art Space on Monday after the police had left."

Lillian interrupted. "Helen said she would take Koranda to a hospital in another town where no one knew him. Leo couldn't do it because another doctor might recognize him. And I was too scared. So Leo and I brought Koranda to the garage at the Art Space and put him in a box there. We had just pulled out of the garage and closed the garage door when Helen called. She was in the restaurant across the street, with Grabowski and you. She said that you had found Koranda. Helen told me to go back into the garage and get Koranda before you and Grabowski got to the garage. So I opened the garage door again, and we put Koranda back into our car, and took him back to the basement of our house."

"Why is he in your car now?" asked Maxine.

"Helen is going to take him to a hospital a long way from Milwaukee," said Leo. "I'll pay Koranda all the money he wants and he won't talk. He needs money for his fishing cottage."

"Yes, Maxine," said a voice in the doorway. Helen stood there. "I'll take care of Koranda. You go home."

"No. Koranda needs an ambulance." Maxine took out her cellphone and called 911. She gave them the information. Then she turned to Leo. "You and I have known each other for years, Leo. Tell me what really happened the night *Musical Chairs* fell on Soren."

"Don't tell her anything," said Helen.

Maxine ignored Helen and kept talking to Dr. Hochstedder. "You knew that Soren wanted to break Lillian's statues at the art show and show everyone the skulls underneath the clay."

Leo sat down on the steps and put his head in his hands. "Soren was a terrible person. He wanted to destroy Lillian's career, and mine."

"And mine," added Helen.

Maxine looked at Leo. "So you decided to stop Soren from breaking Lillian's statues at the show. You cut the rope so the chairs would fall on him. You used a knife from the operating room, didn't you? They're very sharp."

"Yes, I cut the rope," said Leo, "but I didn't want the chairs to fall on Soren. I didn't know he would play the piano all night! I thought that *Musical Chairs* would fall at the beginning of the art show, then Helen would make everyone leave."

"When did you cut the rope?" asked Maxine.

"Right before the show, when Helen, Lillian, and Louie were helping the food company bring in the food. Louie saw me, but I told him I was checking the rope."

"Then you drugged Soren so he would sit at the piano all evening," said Maxine.

"No. I didn't know Soren was drugged!" said Leo.

"When the EMTs took Soren to the ambulance, Soren was breathing much more slowly than normal," said Maxine. "He died because the drug together with the injury made him stop breathing." Maxine looked at Helen. "You drugged Soren, didn't you? You poured his drinks and gave them to Louie. Louie took them to Soren."

Helen smiled. "OK, I put sleeping pills in Soren's drinks. I had to. If Soren broke Lillian's clay heads and showed the skulls underneath, my career would be destroyed! No good artists would want to show their work at the Art Space. I put all my money into the Art Space and the show. I couldn't let Soren ruin me!"

"You also put INH in the chocolates you gave Wyoming," said Maxine. "You wanted him to get sick and not come to the show."

"Yes. I thought Wyoming was Soren's friend, and he would help Soren break Lillian's statues."

"But Wyoming didn't eat the chocolates; Latoya did, and she died," said Maxine. "You called Wyoming to see if he was sick. When he wasn't, you sent some people to shoot him and he almost died."

"Leo arranged that," said Helen.

"Not true, Helen!" shouted Leo. "I told the men to frighten Wyoming so that he wouldn't go out that night. I didn't know they would shoot him!"

"Latoya and Soren died because of both of you," said Maxine.

"Not me!" shouted Helen. "I didn't know that Leo had cut the rope!"

"But you knew the rope was breaking," shouted Lillian. "I told you at the show! Louie told you too!"

"I didn't believe you. The rope was fine before the show," Helen said. "All I wanted was for Soren to stay at the piano all evening so he wouldn't break Lillian's skulls. So I put sleeping pills in his drinks. Leo, you idiot, why didn't you tell me you had cut the rope?"

"Why didn't you tell me you had put sleeping pills in his drink!" shouted Leo. "Then I would have pulled him away from the piano!"

Maxine went on, "After the rope broke and Soren was dead, you realized that Louie had seen Leo cut the rope. Louie also would figure out that you put sleeping pills into Soren's three drinks. And Louie saw Lillian and Leo's Lexus at the Art Space when I was at the restaurant telling Grabowski about the man in the garage. You thought only Louie knew everything, and you know he always talks too much. So you decided to kill Louie by putting sleeping pills into his bottle of allergy pills. You knew he would take a lot. Louie always takes too many pills."

"You can't prove any of this," said Helen. "Leo and Lillian won't tell. And why would the police believe Louie?"

"I believe Louie," said a man's voice. Grabowski was standing in the doorway. "And I can prove many things. I searched your office today, Leo. A lot of INH is missing. And Rolondo has found the people that you paid to shoot Wyoming. I have enough evidence to arrest all three of you for the deaths of Latoya and Soren, for the shooting of Rosa and Wyoming, and for attacking and kidnapping Officer Koranda. The Central Police operator called me when Maxine phoned for an ambulance to come to the Art Space. Open the garage door," Grabowski said to Helen. "The ambulance is outside."

Chapter 19   *Wyoming gets the story*

The next Saturday, Grabowski drove Wyoming Syzinski home from the hospital to his house. Wyoming had agreed to stay with him until he felt stronger. Maxine and Louie were sitting outside on blankets with open picnic baskets. Maxine's blue Taurus X was parked nearby.

Grabowski got out of his rental car and looked at Maxine's Taurus X. "Where did you get that car?" Grabowski demanded.

"From Rolondo's cousin. It's used, but it drives like a dream," replied Maxine.

Grabowski walked slowly around Maxine's car. He opened the doors and looked at the seats. "This looks exactly like my Taurus X that was stolen," he said.

"They all look the same," said Maxine. She handed Grabowski a sandwich.

Wyoming sat down on the blanket next to Maxine. He bit into a tuna sandwich. "I'm still confused about what happened," said Wyoming. "Who shot me?"

"Leo Hochstedder paid two people to shoot you," replied Grabowski, "to keep you away from the Art Space. We arrested them yesterday."

"But why?" asked Wyoming.

"It all started when Lillian Hochstedder lost her sight in one eye," said Maxine. "She couldn't paint well any more, so she tried making statues. She couldn't do that well either."

Wyoming nodded. "In Arizona I tried to teach her how to see with just one eye, but…"

Maxine explained. "So Lillian bought human skulls from Koranda and covered them with clay. People bought them, but unfortunately for her Soren found out. He wanted more money from Helen. When she wouldn't give it to him, or let him take his collection out of the show, Soren decided to destroy her and Lillian. He was going to do it by showing the reporters at the show how Lillian made her skulls."

"Lillian told her husband, Leo," Maxine went on, "who panicked. He didn't want his doctor colleagues and his patients to know that his wife was using real human skulls in her art."

Grabowski continued: "So Leo decided to cut the rope before the show. If *Musical Chairs* fell and broke, Helen could cancel the show. Then Soren wouldn't be able to break Lillian's statues. But Leo didn't tell Helen he had cut the rope."

Maxine took over again: "Helen decided to put sleeping pills into Soren's drinks so that he would be too sleepy to go upstairs and break Lillian's statues. But she didn't tell Leo about the pills. So Soren was sitting at the piano when the chairs fell."

"I still don't understand why Leo hired people to shoot me," insisted Wyoming.

"For the same reason that he and Helen put INH into your chocolates. They thought that you were friends with Soren and that you would help him break open Lillian's statues," said Grabowski. "The gunmen were just trying to frighten you so you would stay inside that night. They weren't supposed to injure you."

"Why was Officer Koranda in the box in the garage?" asked Louie.

Grabowski answered. "Officer Koranda read in the newspaper that Lillian was part of the art show. He came to the show out of curiosity. When he saw the statues, he knew real skulls were inside. He decided he could make some more money. He told Leo Hochstedder that he would tell the newspapers that there were real skulls inside unless Leo gave him a lot of money. They had a fight and Koranda fell down and hit his head."

Maxine took over. "They put Koranda in Leo's Lexus and hid him in their basement. Then Helen said that Grabowski was going to search their house, so they panicked. They drugged him and brought him back to the Art Space garage after the police had left. Helen told them she would take Koranda to a hospital outside Milwaukee where no one knew him. She got you, Louie to leave the garage by telling you that you were needed in south Milwaukee. Then Helen took Grabowski to lunch across the street so he wouldn't see Leo's Lexus. But I found Koranda. So Helen called Lillian on her cellphone, and Leo and Lillian quickly put Koranda back in their Lexus and hid him in their basement again. They decided to take him to his home and pay him to be quiet. Then I found him."

Maxine was thinking. "The night I went to Wyoming's apartment for his art paper, someone hit me on the head."

"Helen hit you," replied Grabowski. "She was searching for the chocolates. The box had her and Leo's fingerprints all over it."

Louie said, "Helen poisoned me because she thought I knew all this."

Grabowski nodded. "You told her that the rope was cut. You knew that you had only given Soren three drinks – not enough to make him so sleepy. You also saw Lillian and Leo's Lexus in the garage on Monday. And you talk too much."

"You solved all the mysteries!" said Louie.

Grabowski looked at Maxine's car. "And I think I even found my stolen Ford Taurus X!"

"This all happened because of money," said Louie. "Rich Dr. Leo Hochstedder was afraid that he would lose his income – his colleagues and his patients – if they found out there were human skulls inside his wife's statues."

"And Soren and Helen both wanted to make a lot of money," said Wyoming.

"And Koranda wanted money to fix up his fishing cottage," added Grabowski.

"Money makes the world go around," said Louie.

"No. Love makes the world go around," said Grabowski. Then he kissed Maxine.